A TASTE OF
QUEBEC

JULIAN ARMSTRONG

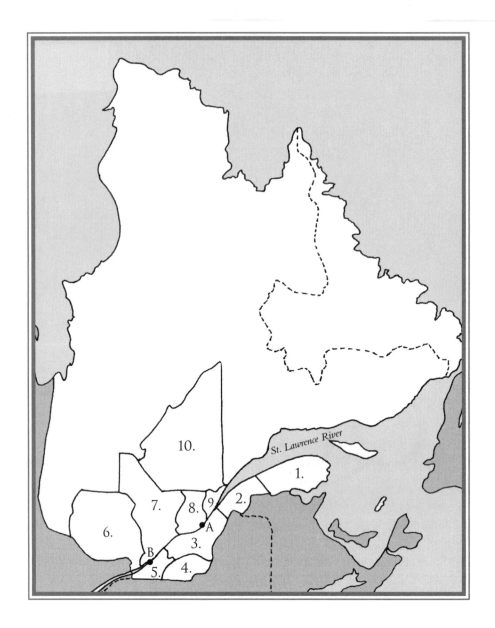

1. GASPÉ

2. BEAUCE

3. CÔTE-DU-SUD

4. EASTERN TOWNSHIPS

5. MONTÉRÉGIE

6. LAURENTIANS-OUTAOUAIS

7. MAURICIE-LANAUDIÈRE

8. QUÉBEC

9. CHARLEVOIX

10. SAGUENAY-LAC SAINT-JEAN

A. QUEBEC CITY

B. MONTREAL

SECOND EDITION

A TASTE OF
QUEBEC

JULIAN ARMSTRONG

MACMILLAN CANADA

TORONTO

First published in Canada in 2001 by
Macmillan Canada, an imprint of CDG Books Canada

Canadian Cataloguing in Publication Data
Armstrong, Julian, 1932–
    A taste of Quebec
2nd ed.
ISBN 1-55335-005-7
1. Cookery, French-Canadian-Quebec style. 2. Cookery-Quebec (Province). I. Title.
TX715.6.A76 2001   641.59714   C2001-930527-3

This book is available at special discounts for bulk purchases by your group or organization for sales promotions, premiums, fundraising and seminars. For details, contact: CDG Books Canada Inc., 99 Yorkville Avenue, Suite 400, Toronto, ON, M5R 3K5. Tel: 416-963-8830. Toll Free: 1-877-963-8830. Fax: 416-923-4821. Web site: cdgbooks.com.

1 2 3 4 5 TRANS 05 04 03 02 01

Cover and text design by Tania Craan

FRONT COVER (clockwise, starting top left)
Foie gras de canard sauce hydromel (Foie gras with honey wine sauce). Courtesy of Tedd Church/ *The Gazette*.
View of the Chateau Frontenac, Quebec City. Courtesy of Jean-Guy Lavoie/Tourisme Quebec.
Soupe au melon (Melon soup). Courtesy of Guillaume Pouliot/ L'Eau à la Bouche
Chef Alain Labrie. Courtesy of Gordon Beck.

SPINE
Auberge Petite Madeleine, Charlevoix. Courtesy of L.M. Renaud/Tourisme Québec

BACK COVER (left to right)
Autumn scenery, Tremblant, Laurentians. Courtesy of Pierre-Phillipe Brunet/Tourisme Québec.
Bas St-Laurent, Ile Verte. Courtesy of Sylvain Majeau/Tourisme Québec
Author photo. Courtesy of Karin Benedict.

Macmillan Canada
An imprint of CDG Books Canada Inc.
Toronto

Printed in Canada

ACKNOWLEDGEMENTS

In the decade since I wrote about Quebec cuisine in my first book, talented chefs and specialty food producers have been pouring their energies into an exciting new movement—to create unique regional cuisines throughout the province. Travellers in "la belle province" are now able to find superb examples of new dishes, new foods, and new beverages wherever they go. My editors at *The Gazette* have my deepest thanks for encouraging my tasting travels: much of the material in this book appeared first, in different form, in the paper's food and travel sections.

To complete this new look at Quebec cuisine, I have leaned heavily on a group of talented people. Suzanne Paré Leclerc, long-time promoter of Quebec's specialty agriculture industry, helped to track down innovators, region by region. Johanna Burkhard, home economist and former *Gazette* columnist, provided advice and recipe expertise. Michelle Gélinas, interpreter of chefs' recipes, cooked her way through many a duxelle and demi-glace to produce home-friendly versions of these regional dishes. *Gazette* photographers took fine pictures and also counselled me on improving my camera skills. Fellow reporter Susan Schwartz spent hours editing various sections. And computer systems technician Robert Ramsey soothed technology panic.

The chefs of Quebec acceded graciously to my repeated requests that they write down their recipes, something they don't ordinarily do. Tourist office staff, government officials, innkeepers, cookbook authors, and fellow Quebec food journalists were endlessly helpful.

I was saddened to learn that many of the older home cooks, who had so hospitably provided me with the traditional dishes of their regions as I worked on the first edition of this book, had died. It was satisfying to learn that their recipes continue to be treasured and used, region by region, for family and holiday gatherings.

This time around, my special thanks go to the following. Quebec City region: Jean Soulard, Suzanne Howard. Saguenay-Lac Saint-Jean: Marcel Bouchard, Daniel Pachon.

Beauce: Cécile Grondin Gamache, Suzanne Vachon. Charlevoix: Eric Bertrand, Jori Smith. Laurentians-Outaouais: Anne Desjardins, Marcel Kretz. Côte-du-Sud: Claude Cyr, Helen Meredith. Gaspé: Michel Morin, Bertrand Major. Montérégie: Alain Pignard, Robert Petch. Mauricie-Lanaudière: Peggy Lafrenière, Micheline Mongrain-Dontigny. Eastern Townships: Robert Gagnon, Pierre Johnston.

At CDG Books, owners of Macmillan, my thanks go to Jennifer Lambert, who shepherded the book from idea to publication; Valerie Adams, who copyedited the manuscript; and Tania Craan, who designed the book.

My family has exhibited patience with my long months at the computer. We're all pleased that, with this book complete, I can now return, notebook and appetite at the ready, to travels along the beautiful roads of my adopted province.

—Julian Armstrong, Montreal, March 2001

CONTENTS

INTRODUCTION

When the word went out across Quebec that some of its finest cheeses might be subject to a health safety ban, I heard about it first from chefs worrying that they might be prevented from serving the delectable soft-ripened raw-milk cheeses in their restaurants. For several weeks, I couldn't go into a cheese shop without being asked to sign a petition protesting federal government interference with Quebec's right to enjoy fine food. I was invited to carry a placard at a public demonstration and watched as the frenzy even halted debate in Quebec's National Assembly.

In my reporting duties as food editor of *The Gazette* of Montreal, I found that government microbiologists agreed such cheese could, if incorrectly aged, cause illness. Food lovers weren't interested. Gastronomic peace was restored only after scientists were persuaded to re-examine the topic. Some cheese makers calmed concerns by labelling their raw-milk cheese—and Quebec's explosion of prize-winning cheeses continued.

Such obsession with good food is a regular part of life everywhere in Quebec. On an island in the St. Lawrence River, I've watched lambs pastured on salt marshes, their shepherds determined to duplicate the pré-salé meat of northern France. Sheltered against a hillside at Saint-André-de-Kamouraska, I've walked in an orchard of heirloom plum trees planted by a family to replicate varieties brought by Récollets priests to New France in the 1600s, and enjoyed the delectable preserves from this fruit. I've jumped out of the way as hundreds of geese rushed out of their barn to feed on the grasses of Baie-du-Febvre farmland, and then feasted on their richly flavoured meat in recipes created by top chefs. In a cellar on Île d'Orléans, I've sipped prize-winning crème de cassis, listening as the wine maker explained how he was working at intensifying the flavour of his black currant liqueur. And, on my favourite of all food quests, I've tracked down an ever-expanding group of bread bakers from Montreal to the Gaspé and from Quebec City to Charlevoix, breaking apart their crusty, chewy loaves to enjoy their succulent bread plain, no butter required.

Food has always been more than just sustenance in Quebec, and the rest of Canada knows it. I'm never surprised to hear that chefs and specialty merchants from coast to coast buy our duck foie gras, farm-raised game meats, smoked fish, maple syrup and—of course—cheese. This food obsession dates back to colonial times, when the first French settlers arrived with their cast-iron pots and pans and began adapting French country cooking to the ingredients of the wilderness.

When I set out to investigate Quebec's culinary past and present, region by region, I had just returned from a food writers' tour of northern France. There I'd seen familiar dishes on menus or in shops—Normandy's spiced pâté called "rillettes" and cider-flavoured chicken, Brittany's fish stews, big paper-thin pancakes and "galettes," and the Champagne region's Flamiche aux poireaux (leek tart) and Tarte au sucre (sugar pie). It was like running into old friends, these original dishes of the earliest settled areas along Quebec's St. Lawrence River. "That's ours," I can remember exclaiming as I stared at a sugar pie in a French village bakery—and immediately realizing that it was theirs first.

Early Quebec cuisine was defined by shortages and by long, cold winters. The time-honoured recipes in this book are economical and simple, calling for few ingredients and long, slow cooking. As the recipes show, the original French dishes—the "tourtières," "ragoûts," and "tartes"—changed as settlers, moving from the old seigneurial lands along the St. Lawrence to new regions, used the local foods they found. The Saguenay, for instance, has a deep-dish tourtière like no other, and the Gaspé is alone in pot-roasting a whole cod to make a "cambuse." Today's progressive chefs are observing the same procedure, basing their creations on the finest, freshest ingredients in their regions.

More than any other part of Canada, Quebec has worked to record its earliest food history. Beginning in 1978, some 30,000 regional dishes were collected from elderly cooks all over the province by the Montreal chefs' training school, the Institut de tourisme et d'hôtellerie du Québec. Many of the cooks were women who had never written down their recipes. Each dish was catalogued, regional differences identified, and a collection published called *Cuisine traditionelle des régions du Québec;* the book has been my bible. Along with a load of maps, producers' directories, and a large cooler for the specialties I invariably find, it accompanies me on all my travels.

For decades, the Quebec government has recognized that good food is good for business. Both the agriculture and tourism departments provide funds and award prizes to chefs, restaurants, and specialty food producers who work to develop a food style in each region of the province. The best chefs don't need such incentives. They're continuously encouraging small, specialty food producers and pressing government officials to reduce the red tape with which food handling and inspection systems in this province are rife. Alain Pignard, the French-born executive chef of Montreal's Queen Elizabeth Hotel, is passionate about "cutting the habit of using big producers. It's like going back to the way it was in Europe, when the little guy would come to my door with his six geese," he told me as he gestured at a delivery of Quebec's latest specialty meat—free-range geese. "Here, everyone wanted to get big," he went on. "In France, the fine food producers don't look to get big, they look to get better. Now, here in Quebec, our producers are learning to stay small." This is not without its challenges. Lamb from the hillsides of the Saguenay region can't be served at Marcel Bouchard's inn at La Baie until it has been trekked to Quebec City, a distance of some 200 kilometres, for slaughter and inspection, and back to the north. Fresh lamb, flown in from New Zealand, can be fresher—and cheaper. And at Métis-sur-Mer, on the edge of the Gaspé, the St. Lawrence River is so wide locals refer to it as "the sea," yet Chef Claude Cyr must cope with the frustration of waiting as fish caught right outside his door must be taken upriver to Rimouski for inspection, then travel back to Cyr's restaurant, losing a day or more of freshness. Marcel described the culinary battle: "We chefs are part of a chain around Quebec. We've been fighting for the last 10 years to give the local producers a chance to commercialize their foods." As he spoke, he held up a basket of beautiful wild mushrooms, filled to over-flowing, just delivered by a supplier down the road.

This book tells of my explorations down many roads as a food journalist in the province I have called home for more than 40 years. I urge you to visit this beautiful land, discover its fascinating history, and enjoy its distinctive regional cuisine. Be assured that, even if your French is limited, you will be welcome at Quebec tables from your first "Bonjour." After all, hospitality is the way we are.

QUÉBEC

Calling Chef Jean Soulard at the Château Frontenac usually means hearing this message: "Je suis dans mes chaudrons..." (I'm cooking). The genial French-born chef is one of the leaders of a movement to encourage the region's specialty food producers. He's often on another line, trying to find enough duck foie gras, wild mushrooms, or the finest crème de cassis (black currant liqueur) for a banquet, or planning his next television show about Quebec's innovations in lamb or goose farming, shrimp or scallop fishing. Jean, a native of La Vendée region of northern France, is a friendly dynamo of a gastronome who believes in encouraging "the little guy," man or woman, so that each dedicated producer continues to make only the best wild-flower honey or raw-milk cheese. He also publishes beautiful collections of his recipes using their foods or beverages. Venturing into his territory to sample, for example, the best French bread in eastern Quebec made by Eric Borderon, or Luc Mailloux's prize-winning soft and succulent raw-milk cheese, Le Chevallier-Mailloux, or superb fruit-flavoured vinegars on Île d'Orléans, I wouldn't dream of a trip to "the ancient capital," as Quebec City is known, without a call to get Jean away from his "chaudrons" (big French cooking pots). Invariably he's ready to describe new delicacies he's found down a country lane, along the St. Lawrence River, or up in the northern hills.

Dining in Quebec City's top restaurants means experiencing regional Quebec cuisine at its best. Spending three evenings in the gastronomically alert company of two chefs—*The Gazette's* restaurant critic Lesley Chesterman and her husband, Montreal pastry chef Bertrand Bazin—I agreed with them that the provincial capital is the place where the message that local is best is being dispensed more devotedly than anywhere else in Quebec, with the possible exception of Charlevoix. Regional cuisine has been endorsed by the city's finest chefs, from Jean Soulard at the Château to Daniel Vézina at Laurie-Raphaël, Yvan Lebrun at L'Initiale, and others. The names of the food producers are often printed right on the chefs' menus, and the cuisine shows it with its fresh, innovative flavours.

All over Le Vieux Québec, as the historic areas of both upper and lower town are called, food and drink is as much a part of the atmosphere as are the 17th and 18th century buildings, and at every price range. The little farmers' market in the old port shows off the finest fruit and vegetables from nearby farms (many on Île d'Orléans), as well as preserves, honey, and vinegars. In upper town, summer means outdoor "terrasse" dining or snacking as you go. One balmy morning, walking from one of the Victorian guest houses on the square behind the Château, I bought a beaver tail, a wide glossy bun available hot in several flavours, from a kiosk on Dufferin Terrace. It was the perfect snack with café-au-lait as I sat on a bench on the boardwalk overlooking the great river, alive with ships and the ferry crossing to Lévis on the south shore. A street musician was playing the flute to a rapt group of tourists. It's such an enchanted city, I began wondering if explorers Jacques Cartier, who arrived in 1535, and Samuel de Champlain, in 1608, were piped ashore.

Under the boardwalk of Dufferin Terrace, as Parks Canada historians Marc Lafrance and Yvon Deloge discovered, were found artifacts to prove that Quebec City has always been a centre for gastronomy. Colonial leaders did not suffer in winter; a greenhouse produced vegetables, and fine wines, olive oil, and spices were on their menus before and after the British conquest in 1759.

One sunny August day I took a food lover's tour of Île d'Orléans, for over three centuries the kind of fertile garden region we now call a microclimate. Nestled between 17th century houses and churches, the latest new agricultural developments are underway, the most impressive being the huge fields of late-season strawberries. With a goal of supplying Quebec with sweet, fresh berries as late as October, agricultural scientist Louis Faucher, working in cooperation with counterparts at the federal agriculture department and McGill University, is beginning production of some new Quebec-bred types, one named Authentique Orléans. Surprises continued when Louis showed me an experimental stand of the magical Far Eastern root ginseng, thriving quietly in a sun-dappled forest. A final garden was secreted on a hillside above the village of Saint-Jean in greenhouses belonging to Fines Herbes par Daniel, the Mirabel grower. Their lemon yellow corn sprouts, miniature bok choy, purslane, and baby romaine lettuce appear on the tables of the region's better restaurants.

PÂTÉ DE FOIE GRAS À L'ANCIENNE

Old-fashioned calves' liver pâté

The Beaupré Coast

Travel the old Avenue Royale (highway 360) east from Montmorency Falls toward Cap-Tourmente and you'll pass some of the earliest farmland of New France, called "beau pré," or beautiful meadow, and have a feast of early Quebec architecture, the old farmhouses angled toward the sun. Stop between L'Ange-Gardien and Château-Richer at a 1695 flour mill called Moulin du Petit-Pré, the first industrial mill to be built in the young colony, and now part of an interpretation centre; 7007 Royal, Château-Richer, (418) 824-3677. Brochures available there (including English) give the history of many of the historic houses along the old road. The shrine of Sainte-Anne-de-Beaupré, both the huge church built in the 1920s and the small 1878 chapel, are sights not to miss. You can complete your trip by dining at La Camarine, a restaurant serving fine regional cuisine; a modern inn is attached; 10947 Sainte-Anne Blvd., Beaupré, (418) 827-1958.

This pâté recipe can be traced back to the traditional cooking of Normandy. Use of the term "foie gras" for this blended preparation troubles classically trained French chefs, who reserve the words for specially fattened goose or duck liver. However, this particular recipe has been in the family of Kathleen Fiset Pineau of Quebec City for a century or more by this name. It is "not recommended for our cholesterol," she once told me.

> 1¼ to 1½ pounds (625 to 750 g) fresh pork fat*
> 3/4 pound (375 g) calves' or goose liver
> 2 cloves garlic, crushed
> 2 tablespoons (30 mL) Cognac or brandy
> ½ teaspoon (2 mL) salt
> Freshly ground pepper
> Pinch each ground nutmeg and dried rosemary
> Truffles (optional)
> 2 or 3 bay leaves

*Do not use salt pork

Using a meat grinder or on–off turns with a food processor, grind or finely chop ¾ pound (375 g) of the pork fat and the liver together. Transfer to a bowl, stir in garlic, Cognac, salt, pepper, nutmeg, and rosemary, mixing well. Cut remaining pork fat into thin strips. Line 2 or 3 small moulds (2 to 3 cups/500 to 750 mL) with some of the strips of fat. Place a truffle, if desired, and a bay leaf in each mould. Add liver mixture and cover with more strips of the fat. Place moulds in a shallow roasting pan and add 1 inch (2.5 cm) of boiling water in the bottom of pan.

Place in 325°F (160°C) oven and oven-poach for 2 to 3 hours, depending on size of moulds, or until mixture is set in the centre. Let cool, then refrigerate. Serve cold as a spread on crackers or toast.

Makes about 2 pounds (1 kg) pâté

TIP: Pâté may be made 10 days ahead and stored, covered, in the refrigerator.

PÂTE AUX POIREAUX

Leek tart

This leek and cheese quiche from Île d'Orléans is related to the "Flamiche aux poireaux," a savoury leek tart made in northern France and Flanders. The recipe can also be used to make small tarts.

> 6 tablespoons (90 mL) butter
> 4 to 5 leeks, white and light green part only, finely chopped
> ½ cup (125 mL) water
> 2 tablespoons (30 mL) all-purpose flour
> Salt and freshly ground pepper
> 1 egg
> 2 tablespoons (30 mL) light cream
> 1 cup (250 mL) mild Cheddar cheese, grated
> 9-inch (23 cm) tart shell lined with pastry (use half of dough, recipe p. 15)

In a large, heavy saucepan, heat 4 tablespoons (60 mL) of the butter over medium-low heat and cook leeks, stirring often, for 10 minutes. Add water, cover, and simmer gently for 20 to 25 minutes or until very tender.

In a saucepan, melt the remaining 2 tablespoons (30 mL) butter over medium heat; stir in flour and cook until bubbly. Blend in leek mixture and bring to a boil; season with salt and pepper. Remove from heat and let cool slightly.

In a bowl, beat egg with cream and stir into leek mixture. Pour into unbaked tart shell. Sprinkle evenly with cheese. Bake in a preheated 400°F (200°C) oven for 25 to 30 minutes or until cheese begins to brown.

Six servings

The Onion Family

A green onion is a scallion or an "échalote" but not a shallot, according to Quebec's Office de la langue française. The shallot is the small reddish-skinned onion used to season so many French dishes. Onions, a favourite Quebec food, were traditionally grown in such quantities in the area of Beauport, north of Quebec City, that farmers used to be nicknamed "les oignons de Beauport." On Île d'Orléans, leeks are a continuing favourite, and island farmers are still dubbed "les poireaux" because of their fondness for this vegetable.

CRÊPES À NICOLE

Potato pancakes

The potato, Quebec's top vegetable, is grown in such large quantities around Saint-Ubalde, northwest of Quebec City, that the Club optimiste de Saint-Ubalde published a collection of more than 200 recipes using the vegetable. Marie Claire Cauchon, who persuaded cooks of all ages to part with their favourites, rated these crêpes as one of Saint-Ubalde's best-liked dishes.

> 2 cups (500 mL) peeled, grated raw potatoes
> 2 tablespoons (30 mL) minced onion
> 2 tablespoons (30 mL) all-purpose flour
> ½ teaspoon (2 mL) baking powder
> ½ teaspoon (2 mL) salt, or to taste
> Pinch freshly ground pepper
> 2 eggs, lightly beaten
> Oil for frying

In a bowl, combine potatoes, onion, flour, baking powder, salt, and pepper. Stir in eggs. Heat enough oil to coat the bottom of a crêpe pan or heavy frying pan over medium-high heat. Drop batter by tablespoonfuls (15 mL) into hot oil and fry crêpes 2 minutes per side or until golden. Keep crêpes warm while cooking remaining batter. Serve hot.

Four servings

China Pie

A meat pie named "pâté chinois" is found on menus in small, family-style Quebec restaurants. It has no connection with Chinese cuisine. It's a French-Canadian term for shepherd's pie, the combination of ground-up cooked meat, gravy, and mashed potatoes. The name was traced by Quebec food historian Claude Poirier to a town in the state of Maine called China. In the late 19th century, thousands of Quebecers migrated to the northeastern United States to work in the mills. Those who settled in the town of China eventually returned to Quebec with a recipe for shepherd's pie, which they called "pâté chinois."

HOMARD AU PAPRIKA HARICOT BLANCS À L'HUILE D'ÉPICES

Lobster with spiced white beans

Brittany-born Chef Yvan Lebrun and Maître d'hôtel Rolande Leclerc have created a quiet oasis of gastronomy in an old bank in Quebec City's lower town for their restaurant L'Initiale. It's the perfect setting to enjoy such luxurious dishes as this one of lobster with beans seasoned with a spiced vinaigrette. The lobster could be replaced with fillets of any white fish, dipped in flour and fried in butter.

> 1 cup (250 mL) white French lingo beans or
>   small dry white beans
> ½ cup (125 mL) diced carrots
> ½ cup (125 mL) chopped leeks
> Bouquet garni*
> Freshly ground pepper and salt
> ¼ teaspoon (1 mL) grated fresh or ground turmeric
> ¼ teaspoon (1 mL) each whole cumin,
>   caraway seeds, and fennel seeds
> 1 teaspoon (5 mL) crushed white peppercorns
> 6 tablespoons (90 mL) grape seed oil or
>   sunflower oil
> ¼ vanilla bean, split
> Grated rind of 1 lemon
> 2 tablespoons (30 mL) cider vinegar
> 4 lobsters, 1¼ pounds (625 g) each
> 1 tablespoon (15 mL) butter
> ½ teaspoon (2 mL) mild paprika
> 2 tablespoons (30 mL) chopped chives

*One sprig thyme, bay leaf, and parsley stem with leaves tied in a cheesecloth bag

Rinse beans; place in a large saucepan and cover with cold water. Bring to a boil, reduce heat, and simmer for 5 minutes. Remove from heat and let stand for 1 hour. Add carrots, leeks, bouquet garni, ground pepper and salt. Return to a boil; reduce heat, partially cover, and cook until beans are tender, about 1 hour. Drain; season with salt to taste and set aside.

In a saucepan, gently toast turmeric, cumin, caraway, fennel and crushed white peppercorns over medium heat, stirring, until fragrant. Let cool slightly. Grind spices in a clean coffee grinder or crush, using a mortar and pestle. In a small saucepan, heat oil over low heat until lukewarm. Add toasted spices, vanilla bean, and lemon rind. Place over very low heat for 5 minutes to infuse flavours; strain through a fine sieve into a bowl. Let cool slightly; add vinegar and set aside.

Immerse lobsters in a large pot of boiling, salted water and cook for 4 minutes. Drain and run under cold water to chill. Remove meat from shells and cut into bite-sized pieces.

In a large frying pan, heat butter over medium-high heat and cook lobster just until heated through; sprinkle with paprika. In a large saucepan, combine spiced vinaigrette and beans and cook, stirring, until heated through; sprinkle with chives. Spoon beans on 4 warmed serving plates and top with lobster; serve at once.

Four servings

TIP: Cook beans up to 3 days in advance and refrigerate. Prepare vinaigrette and cook lobsters up to 3 hours ahead.

BOEUF À L'ANCIENNE AU VIN ROUGE

Île de Bacchus

Explorer Jacques Cartier originally named Île d'Orleans for the god of wine after he saw grapevines on its lush slopes in 1535. Both a cheese maker and winery on the island use the name Bacchus. Six villages line its shores. At Saint-Pierre is Ferme Monna, where Bernard Monna (photo opposite) makes his black currants into superb apéritifs, wines, and liqueurs, and Domaine Steinbach, where Belgian-born Philippe Steinbach uses his apples to make cider, vinegar, and mustard. Another island vinegar selling in stores and kiosks is Les Vinaigres à l'Ancienne de l'Île d'Orléans. Good regional cuisine is served at Le Canard Huppé in the village of Saint-Laurent, also home to Ferme Orléans, where a variety of game birds are raised and sold. Also at Saint-Laurent is La Forge à Pique-Assaut, an old-time forge demonstrating iron-working. A sweet finale is Chocolaterie de l'Île d'Orléans at Sainte-Pétronille.

Old-fashioned beef in red wine

Suzanne Howard, who ran a restaurant she called L'Âtre (the hearth) at Sainte-Famille on Île d'Orléans for 40 years, found this recipe in *The Art of Cookery Made Easy*, an 1869 cookbook in the library of the Ursulines' convent in Quebec City. She served this rustic version of boeuf bourguignon in the restaurant for many years. The old cookbook offered this tip: "Note that you must take great care in doing your beef this way that your fire is low." Serve with a salad, either tossed greens or sliced tomatoes with capers.

2 pounds (1 kg) lean boneless beef chuck or rump,
    cut in 2-inch (5 cm) cubes
1½ cups (375 mL) dry red wine
4 tablespoons (60 mL) vegetable oil
2 shallots, finely chopped
1 small carrot, finely chopped
1 onion, sliced
3 tablespoons (45 mL) butter
Bouquet garni*
2 tablespoons (30 mL) all-purpose flour
1 cup (250 mL) beef stock
1 tablespoon (15 mL) tomato paste
2 cloves garlic, finely chopped
1 teaspoon (5 mL) dried savory
½ teaspoon (2 mL) dried thyme
Salt and freshly ground pepper
20 white pearl onions, peeled
4 carrots, peeled, sliced
4 medium potatoes, peeled, cubed
½ pound (250 g) small white mushrooms, left whole
2 tablespoons (30 mL) finely chopped parsley

* Three parsley sprigs and a bay leaf tied in a cheesecloth bag

In a bowl, combine beef cubes with wine, 1 tablespoon (15 mL) of the oil, shallots, carrots, and onion. Let marinate 8 to 24 hours in refrigerator. Remove meat from marinade and pat meat dry with paper towels. Strain marinade; reserve both marinade and vegetables. In a large, heavy frying pan, heat remaining oil and 1 tablespoon (15 mL) of the butter over high heat. Cook beef cubes, in batches, until browned on all sides. Using a slotted spoon, transfer beef to a casserole dish with a cover. Bury the bouquet garni in the meat.

Add reserved vegetables to frying pan, and cook, stirring, for 5 minutes or until lightly browned. Sprinkle with flour (add a little oil if mixture appears dry). Cook, stirring, until flour is lightly coloured. Pour in beef stock, reserved wine marinade, and tomato paste. Bring to a boil, stirring constantly, scraping up any brown bits from bottom of pan, until sauce thickens. Stir in garlic, savory, thyme, and salt and pepper to taste; pour sauce over beef. Sauce should almost cover the meat; add more beef stock or wine if necessary. Cover casserole and bake in a 350°F (180°C) oven for 1½ hours.

Heat remaining 2 tablespoons (30 mL) butter in large frying pan over medium heat and cook pearl onions, stirring, for 2 minutes or until lightly coloured. Add onions, carrots, and potatoes to casserole and return to oven for 20 to 25 minutes or until vegetables are just tender. Add mushrooms to frying pan; cook, stirring, for 3 minutes. Add to casserole and cook for 5 to 10 minutes more or until meat and vegetables are tender.

To serve, remove bouquet garni and sprinkle with chopped parsley.

Six to eight servings

RAGOÛT DE PETITES BOULETTES ET DE PATTES DE COCHON

Meatball and pork hocks stew

The Three Sisters

The native peoples of Quebec introduced the French settlers to new foods, beginning with maple syrup. Their three vegetables became part of the "habitant" diet. Corn they named "blé d'inde," (Indian corn), a term used to this day interchangeably with "maïs sucré" (sweet corn). Squash included the pumpkin, which explorer Jacques Cartier thought was a melon. Marie de l'Incarnation, who founded the Ursuline order in Quebec City, sent seeds of "citrouilles des Iroquois" (Iroquois pumpkins) back to France in 1668, plus tips on how to fry this vegetable, make it into a cream soup, bake it in the oven like apples, or braise it like pears. Beans were the third vegetable. The Indians grew this trio together in mounds, corn in the centre, beans supported by the corn, and squash around the other two so their vines would control the weeds. The Iroquois called this trio the three sisters. Native artists depict them together to this day.

Slow, careful cooking gives this time-honoured dish a rich flavour despite its humble ingredients. It was served frequently at L'Âtre (the hearth), a one-time restaurant at Sainte-Famille on Île d'Orléans. Owner Suzanne Howard designed her menu in keeping with her 1680 stone farmhouse. She liked to serve the stew with miniature potato pancakes and pickled beets and cucumbers.

> 2 pork hocks (1½ pounds/750 g)
> ¼ cup (60 mL) all-purpose flour
> Salt and freshly ground pepper
> 2 tablespoons (30 mL) butter
> 2 carrots
> 1 stalk celery
> 2 medium onions, quartered
> 1 bay leaf

Dredge pork hocks in flour seasoned with salt and pepper. In a large, heavy frying pan, heat butter over high heat and brown pork on all sides to a rich, golden brown. Transfer to a large, heavy saucepan and add enough water to cover the meat. Add carrots, celery, onions, and bay leaf. Season with salt and pepper to taste. Bring to a boil, skim off any foam that forms on top, and simmer until meat is tender, about 1½ to 2 hours.

Remove pork and transfer to cutting board. Remove meat from bones, discarding skin and fat. Cut meat into pieces; set aside. Strain stock and return to saucepan; add bones to stock and simmer gently for 2 more hours. Skim off fat, strain and reduce stock over medium heat to about 4 cups (1 L); set aside.

Meatballs

1 pound (500 g) ground veal
2 pounds (1 kg) ground pork
¼ cup (60 mL) chopped fresh parsley
3 cloves garlic, minced
2 slices dry (or stale) bread, crumbled
¼ teaspoon (1 mL) ground cloves
Pinch ground allspice
Salt and freshly ground pepper
2 tablespoons (30 mL) butter
2 tablespoons (30 mL) vegetable oil
¼ cup (60 mL) dry white wine

In a large bowl, combine veal, pork, parsley, garlic, crumbled bread, cloves, allspice, salt, and pepper to taste; mix well. Shape into meatballs, about 1 inch (2.5 cm) in diameter.

In a large, heavy frying pan, heat butter and oil over medium-high heat and cook meatballs in batches until browned on all sides. Transfer to a large, heavy flameproof casserole dish or large saucepan. Discard fat in frying pan and add wine. Place over medium heat, scraping up any brown bits from bottom of pan. Add to meatballs along with reserved pork stock. Cover and cook over medium-low heat for 30 minutes. Add reserved cooked pork and simmer gently for 30 minutes more.

Eight to ten servings

TIP: The pork hocks may be cooked and the stock simmered the day before. Refrigerate the dish. Three hours before serving time, skim off fat, reheat dish gently, then add meatballs and complete dish. Freezes well for up to one month; thaw in the refrigerator.

TOURTIÈRE DE QUÉBEC

Quebec pork pie

Tourtière

Food historians like to explain the name of Quebec's meat pie, some tracing it to the French cooking utensil of the same name, others to a passenger pigeon called the "tourte" or "oiseau blanc," which was plentiful in eastern Canada into the 20th century. The birds, gamey in flavour like grouse or pheasant, were unafraid of man, Montrealer Louis Amos told me, quoting his grandfather. If farmers scattered corn on a field, a flock would come to feed and it would be possible to kill them with clubs or trap them under a net. The birds could be plucked, cleaned, and preserved in brine for winter meals, and sometimes mixed with pork, beef, and seasonings to make a tourtière. Around 1920, so his story goes, a severe storm blew the last flock of the birds out to sea, never to return. "That's the folklore," he said.

This tourtière recipe is the region's traditional pork and vegetable pie. A family recipe belonging to Kathleen Fiset Pineau of Quebec City, it was one of the winners of a 1984 tourtière contest conducted by *The Gazette* of Montreal. Mme Pineau originally obtained the recipe from an aunt who lived on the south shore of the St. Lawrence River. She called it the Quebec City style of tourtière; the use of rolled oats instead of potatoes to thicken the filling shows a Scottish influence.

> 1¼ pounds (625 g) ground pork
> ½ to ¾ cup (125 to 175 mL) cold water
> ½ cup (125 mL) finely chopped onion
> ¼ cup (60 mL) finely chopped celery
> ½ teaspoon (2 mL) ground black pepper
> 1 bay leaf
> ½ teaspoon (2 mL) dried savory
> ¼ teaspoon (1 mL) dried rosemary
> ¼ teaspoon (1 mL) grated nutmeg
> Pinch cinnamon
> Salt
> ¼ cup (60 mL) old-fashioned rolled oats
> Pastry for double-crust, 9-inch (23 cm) pie
>   (recipe follows)

In a large, heavy saucepan, combine pork with ½ cup (125 mL) cold water and heat to boiling point, stirring to break up lumps of meat. Stir in onion, celery, pepper, bay leaf, savory, rosemary, nutmeg, and cinnamon. Cook, covered, over medium-low heat for 1¼ hours, adding up to another ¼ cup (50 mL) water if mixture dries out. Halfway through cooking time, season with salt to taste. Stir in rolled oats and cook, stirring, for 1 to 2 minutes. Remove bay leaf. Let cool.

Meanwhile, line a 9-inch (23 cm) pie plate with pastry. Spoon meat mixture into pie shell and cover with remaining pastry. Trim and crimp edges to seal; cut steam vents in top crust. Decorate as desired. Bake in preheated 425°F (220°C) oven for 15 minutes; reduce heat to 375°F (190°C) and bake another 25 minutes or until crust is golden.

Six servings

TIP: The unbaked tourtière may be frozen for up to a month. Thaw in the refrigerator and bake as directed.

Pastry

Make pastry for a 2-crust, 8-inch (20 cm) to 10-inch pie using shortening or lard. (For additional flavour, substitute butter for part of the fat.) In a bowl, mix 2 cups (500 mL) sifted all-purpose flour with ¼ teaspoon (1 mL) salt. With pastry blender or 2 knives, cut in ¾ cup (175 mL) chilled, cubed fat until mixture resembles coarse crumbs. Measure ¼ to ⅓ cup (60 to 75 mL) ice water. Sprinkle over mixture, a spoonful at a time, stirring with a fork, adding just enough water so dough holds together. Shape into a ball, press into a flat disc, wrap in plastic wrap and chill for 1 hour. Leftover pastry can be frozen for later use.

CONFITURE AIGRE-DOUCE

Fruit vegetable relish

This colourful chutney-type relish was served with tourtière at L'Âtre, the one-time restaurant in Sainte Famille on Île d'Orléans. Proprietress Suzanne Howard always made a big batch at harvest time.

3 onions, chopped
1 stalk celery, chopped
2 green peppers, coarsely chopped
6 tomatoes, peeled and chopped
6 peaches, peeled and coarsely chopped, or 1 can
   (19 ounces/540 mL), coarsely chopped
6 apples, peeled, cored, and coarsely chopped
6 pears, peeled, cored, and coarsely chopped
2 cups (500 mL) cider vinegar
1½ cups (375 mL) granulated sugar
3 tablespoons (45 mL) coarse salt
4 teaspoons (20 mL) pickling spices, tied in a
   cheesecloth bag

In a large, heavy stainless steel saucepan, combine onions, celery, peppers, tomatoes, peaches, apples, pears, vinegar, sugar, salt, and spice bag. Bring to a boil over high heat; reduce heat and simmer, uncovered, for about 1 hour or until thickened and reduced. Remove spice bag; ladle relish into hot, sterilized jars and seal using 2-piece lids.

Makes 3 to 4 one-pint (500 mL) jars

The Story of Honey

Swarms of bees at work in the Musée de l'Abeille (bee museum) in Château-Richer have a long history of making what is mankind's first sugar. These insects were found in Egyptian tombs, their honey used to embalm the bodies of the pharaohs. Bees became the emblem of French kings, and, after a death in France, peasants would cover their hives with a mourning veil. Unknown in North America until Europeans imported them to Massachusetts in about 1630, they appeared in Canada only after the American Revolution. The museum, in an institutional building on highway 138, caters to every age, including an explanation of styles of hives, a tasting of different honeys, and a shop selling every conceivable honeyed treat. Admission charge. 8862 Sainte-Anne Blvd., Château-Richer, (418) 824-4411; www.musee-abeille.qc.ca

FILETS DE CORÉGONE AU PORTO

Whitefish with port sauce

Chef Jean Soulard of the Château Frontenac in Quebec City likes his fish simply cooked with a little port wine, and then served with a creamy sauce and steamed vegetables.

4 fillets whitefish or sole (1 pound/500 g)
1 large shallot, finely chopped
½ cup (125 mL) red port wine
½ cup (125 mL) dry white wine
¼ cup (60 mL) white vermouth
½ cup (125 mL) fish stock
Salt and freshly ground white pepper
1 cup (250 mL) whipping cream
8 ounces (250 g) fresh, multicoloured or
   spinach noodles

Arrange fish fillets in a single layer in a shallow, buttered baking pan. Sprinkle with shallot; pour port, white wine, vermouth, and fish stock over fillets. Season with salt and pepper. Cover with parchment paper or aluminum foil and bake in preheated 375°F (190°C) oven for 8 to 10 minutes or just until fish turns opaque. Remove fish to a heated platter and keep warm. Pour juices into a medium saucepan and bring to a boil; cook until reduced to ¾ cup (175 mL). Stir in cream and cook until slightly reduced and sauce coats a wooden spoon. Season with salt and pepper to taste.

Meanwhile, cook noodles in a large pot of boiling, salted water until al dente (tender but firm). Transfer to a large bowl. Pour half of the sauce over noodles and toss. Ladle pasta into 4 warmed shallow bowls; top with fish fillets and spoon remaining sauce over. Serve with steamed fresh vegetables.

Four servings

Where to Stay

Quebec City is rich in hotels, beginning with the luxurious castle called the Château Frontenac, which has dominated upper town physically and socially since it opened in 1893; 1 des Carrières St.; (418) 692-3861, (800) 441-1414. In the restored lower town, Auberge Saint-Antoine, opened in 1992 in an 1830s warehouse, is comfortable and expensive; 10 Saint-Antoine St.; (418) 692-2211, (800) 267-0525. On the western tip of Île d'Orléans at Sainte-Pétronille is the recently rebuilt and charming Auberge La Goéliche, with a spectacular view of the St. Lawrence and Quebec City and moderate rates; (418) 828-2248, (888) 511-2248; www.oricom.ca/aubergela-goeliche. Near the hotel is the one-time studio of 19th century Ontario-born painter Horatio Walker, who spent much of his career painting the habitant life of his beloved island.

TARTE DU MANOIR
AUX DATTES ET AUX NOIX

Country-style date nut pie

This rich, strongly flavoured dessert is one of the favourites on the menu at Restaurant aux Anciens Canadiens in Quebec City. This restaurant, located in two houses dating back to 1675, specializes in lightened versions of the earliest Quebec dishes. The tradition of cooking with dried fruit goes back to colonial times.

½ cup (125 mL) butter, at room temperature
1 cup (250 mL) packed brown sugar
4 eggs
1 teaspoon (5 mL) cinnamon
½ teaspoon (2 mL) ground nutmeg
1 teaspoon (5 mL) vanilla extract
¾ cup (175 mL) whipping cream
½ cup (125 mL) chopped dates
½ cup (125 mL) raisins
½ cup (125 mL) chopped walnuts
Single-crust, 9-inch (23 cm) pie shell lined with
   pastry (recipe p. 15)

In a bowl, cream butter with brown sugar until fluffy. Beat in eggs, 1 at a time, until incorporated. Stir in cinnamon, nutmeg, vanilla, and cream until smooth. Stir in dates, raisins, and nuts. Pour filling into pastry-lined pie shell. Bake in a preheated 350°F (180°C) oven for 45 minutes or until top is set and lightly browned.

Eight servings

TIP: Pastry may be prepared, rolled out to line pan, and refrigerated, covered, for several hours.

CÔTE-DU-SUD

The oldest shores of Quebec, haunts of Basque fishermen as early as the 16th century, are home to new food experiments linked to France. One site is Île Verte, an island in the St. Lawrence River off Rivière-du-Loup, where lambs are being raised on the salty marsh grasses. Another area is at Baie-du-Febvre, a one-time seigneury near Nicolet, where an unusual white goose is being raised on farms in a region known as a major resting area for wild birds. Both developments are the talk of top chefs. The lamb, modelled on the pré-salé meat of Brittany and Normandy, is snapped up each fall by chefs such as Jean Soulard of the Château Frontenac in Quebec City and Normand Laprise of Montreal's Restaurant Toqué! Laprise refers to this new meat as "a wow" of a food. The goose is rated so highly that it was smoked and served to celebrated French chef Paul Bocuse when he came to dine at Montreal's Queen Elizabeth Hotel.

The new lamb carries no hint of salt, tasting only like the most flavourful, most tender meat you've ever eaten. It's the brainchild of two agricultural scientists, Jacques DeBlois and Mathieu Clotteau, who led me to see their flock of 100 lambs one August morning. I stood on the edge of the marshy shore, my ears filled with the sound of crunching as the animals bit down on their diet of crisp, naturally salty, marsh grasses. These animals could not be reared anywhere else on the St. Lawrence, the producers explained, because upstream waters are not salty enough to produce the same plants and, downstream, the tides dissipate, and the grasses are too sparse. Next step, Jacques told me, is to get government approval for a lamb "contrôlée" stamp along the lines of the "appellation contrôlée" identification on wine. Lamb was not an original taste with the early settlers, who raised sheep for wool, not meat. But helped by an increasing number of lamb producers and the imaginative lamb-cooking of better chefs, the meat is becoming a delicacy throughout Quebec.

Goose has a big name along the river, for hunters congregate each fall to shoot snow geese on the shores and islands. This bird and wild duck and partridge turn up in the simplest family recipes, along with deer and moose. The regional "cipâte" (or "cipaille") and tourtière are best made with wild meats.

As you travel along the old shore highway, you'll see some of the oldest and best-preserved houses, mills, and churches of the past three centuries. As the river widens, becomes salty and tidal, and therefore begins to be called "the sea," and the blue hills of northern Quebec recede on the horizon, you'll see more islands offshore. One is called Île aux Basques, where you can find ruins of the fireplaces in which Basque fishermen rendered whale oil as early as 1584. Trois-Pistoles, an old town dominated by one of the most extravagant and beautiful churches in Quebec, has a museum called the Parc de l'aventure basque en Amérique that explains whale-hunting of those early times.

Centuries-old fishing practices can be found along this shore. Fish has always been a favoured food in this region. Montreal home economist Suzanne Paré Leclerc, who was born and raised in Trois-Pistoles, remembers eating fish three or four times a week in summer and almost as often in winter. Fish of all species are smoked, and eel and sturgeon fished as they were in colonial times. You'll see eel weirs stretching out from shore, and Kamouraska has an eel interpretation centre to explain the catching and handling of this long, snakelike fish, now mostly exported to Europe.

Soeur Monique Chevrier—the gastronomical nun and cookbook author who once ran a successful Montreal cooking school—traces the cooking traditions of the Côte-du-Sud back to Quebec's top domestic science school, which was started in 1905 in Saint-Pascal-de-Kamouraska. Her order, Congrégation de Notre-Dame, sent her there to teach cooking from 1947 to 1955, at the Institution Chanoine-Beaudet. The school attracted girls from as far away as Lac Saint-Jean and Gaspé for a four-year course that was designed to teach the basics of traditional Quebec cuisine. "Technique was not a grand affair," the nun told me, recalling that, at first, students, who came mostly from farms, were accustomed to wood stoves. "We taught on wood," said Soeur Monique.

Food preservation techniques were a big part of the course. She would teach how to store root vegetables in sand for the winter and how to wrap green tomatoes in paper and keep them in a cool, humid cellar. "You could be eating fresh, ripe tomatoes into February with this method," she said.

The order's major contribution to passing on culinary traditions was its basic cookbook, *La cuisine raisonnée,* published in 1919. It went through 11 editions, selling over a million copies, until the final 1985 version, in metric measures. The role of the book cannot be overestimated, in Soeur Monique's opinion: "It was the cookbook that influenced every woman in the province. To this day, it represents Quebec family cooking."

French country cooking styles persist in the region's cooking. The late Edith Martin, studying the family recipes of Trois-Pistoles, identified dishes of both northwestern France and Alsace. Winter tarts are made in the French manner, she told me. "Just the plain fruit in a pastry shell with none of the American touches such as custard or meringue." And cakes are flavoured with dried fruits such as raisins and prunes, and nuts, particularly hazelnuts.

LA FEUILLANTINE DE CHÈVRE

Goat cheese tartlets with salad greens and sun-dried tomato vinaigrette

Patrick Gonfond, chef at La Coureuse des Grèves, a little restaurant in Saint-Jean-Port-Joli, makes cheese-filled tartlets with chèvre cheese from Fromagerie Cayer, a cheese maker across the St. Lawrence River at Saint-Raymond-de-Portneuf. He serves it with a sun-dried tomato vinaigrette, endive and exotic salad greens.

2 sheets phyllo pastry
6 tablespoons (90 mL) unsalted butter, melted
4 ounces (125 g) fresh goat cheese, at room temperature
¼ cup (60 mL) whipping cream
2 tablespoons (30 mL) apricot jam
Sun-dried Tomato Vinaigrette (recipe follows)
2 cups (500 mL) oak-leaf lettuce or exotic salad greens
1 endive, separated into leaves

Place 1 sheet of phyllo pastry on work surface and brush lightly with melted butter. Top with second sheet of phyllo and brush again with melted butter. Cut pastry into 4 equal squares. Using a medium muffin pan (cups hold ⅓ cup/75 mL filling each), butter 4 of the muffin cups and line with the phyllo squares, shaping the top of the pastry out from the edges like flower petals. Bake pastry in oven preheated to 400°F (200°C) for 3 to 4 minutes, or just until golden brown and crisp. Let cool.

In a bowl, combine the remaining melted butter, goat cheese, and cream until smooth. In a small saucepan, add about 1 teaspoon (5 mL) water to the apricot jam and heat until melted. Brush inside of each baked pastry shell with the jam. Just before serving, arrange pastry shells on 4 serving plates. Spoon about ¼ cup (60 mL) of the cheese mixture into each pastry shell. Surround with endive leaves and salad greens. Drizzle sun-dried tomato vinaigrette over tartlets and greens; serve at once.

Four servings

Sun-dried Tomato Vinaigrette
1/2 cup (125 mL) sun-dried tomatoes in oil
¼ cup (60 mL) balsamic vinegar
¼ cup (60 mL) white wine
3 medium shallots, finely chopped
Salt and freshly ground pepper

Drain tomatoes, reserving enough oil to measure 6 tablespoons (90 mL). Place oil, vinegar, wine, and shallots in food processor or blender. Start blending ingredients, adding the tomatoes one at a time and blending until mixture is smooth and light. Season with salt and pepper to taste.

TIP: The tart shells, cheese mixture, and tomato sauce may each be prepared several hours in advance. Assemble dish only at the last minute.

LES PÉTONCLES À LA NAGE

Scallop soup

Claude Cyr, chef-proprietor of Au Coin de la Baie in Métis-sur-Mer, has been a leader in Quebec's regional cuisine movement for decades. A specialist in fish, he makes this simple soup from scallops and vegetables. The heat of the hot stock serves to cook the scallops.

> 1 cup (250 mL) dry white wine
> 1 cup (250 mL) Fish Stock (recipe follows)
> ¼ cup (60 mL) each fine julienned strips of carrots, turnips, and leeks
> Salt and freshly ground white pepper
> 12 large fresh scallops

In a medium stainless steel saucepan, bring wine, fish stock, and vegetables to a boil; season with salt and pepper to taste. Reduce heat and simmer for 5 minutes or until vegetables are tender–crisp. Place 6 scallops in each of 2 heated bowls. Ladle the very hot stock over the scallops and stir; serve at once.

Two servings

Fish Stock

2 pounds (1 kg) fish heads, bones, and trimmings[*]
8 cups (2 L) water[**]
1 onion, sliced
1 carrot, chopped
1 celery stalk, chopped
3 parsley stems
1 bay leaf
Salt and freshly ground white pepper

[*] Bones from mild-flavoured varieties such as halibut, sole, and cod are recommended.

[**] Or use 1 cup (250 mL) white wine for 1 cup (250 mL) of the water.

In a stockpot or large saucepan, place fish trimmings, water, onion, carrot, celery, parsley, and bay leaf; season with salt and pepper. Bring to a boil, partially cover, and reduce heat. Simmer for 30 to 40 minutes. Strain stock through a cheesecloth-lined sieve into a bowl. Let cool.

Makes about 6 cups (1.5 L)

TIP: Fish stock may be made and vegetables cut up in advance.

Rosy Lake

The most spectacular fall harvest in Quebec is of cranberries, and the biggest cranberry bogs, at Saint-Louis-de-Blandford, midway between Montreal and Quebec City, are open to visitors for a month, beginning in late September. A project of the Bieler family, the Cranberry Interpretation Centre explains that when these bitter red cousins of the blueberry ripen, the bogs in which they grow are flooded with water so the cranberries can be scooped up mechanically. Mostly sold fresh, frozen, or made into juice, the berries also make unusual preserves. Tastings are part of the visitors' tour, offered Tuesday through Sunday from 10 a.m. to 5 p.m. The address is 320 Rang Saint-François, off autoroute 20 at exit 235, then south on highway 263. For information, call (819) 364-5112.

CIPAILLE

Layered meat pie

Architectural Treasures

The St. Lawrence River shore offers
an architectural feast for the eyes,
including a variety of roofs on 19th
century clapboard farmhouses. The
most distinctive has the so-called
Kamouraska roof, a pronounced
concave curve starting just under
the eave and dipping down to the
wall of the house. It's a style
explained by the fact that carpen-
ters were also boat-builders. La
Pocatière has a spectacular old
seminary on a height of land, and
the ethnology museum, Musée
François-Pilote, which includes
1860 interiors, antique sleighs, and
buggies. At Saint-Denis is the
Maison Chapais, the 1834 residence of Jean-Charles Chapais,
one of the fathers of Confederation.
In Kamouraska, the old courthouse
(1888) and museum (1851) tell the
history of riverside life. Rivière-du-
Loup has a "heritage walk," which
includes the restored Manoir Fraser,
a Victorian mansion dating from
1830, inhabited by William Fraser,
the last seigneur of the region. The

This traditional layered pie is best made with game, say cooks in
the region. Failing a supply of venison or pheasant, you can make
"cipaille," or "cipâte" as it's often called, with a mixture of meats
and poultry. This recipe belongs to Gisèle Beaulieu of Trinité-des-
Monts on the Rimouski River.

> 2 pounds (1 kg) boneless chicken, such as breasts
>   and thighs
> 2 pounds (1 kg) lean stew beef
> 2 pounds (1 kg) lean pork
> 4 onions, coarsely chopped
> ¼ pound (125 g) salt pork, thinly sliced
> 2 cups (500 mL) peeled, cubed potatoes
> 1 teaspoon (5 mL) salt
> ½ teaspoon (2 mL) freshly ground pepper
> ¼ teaspoon (1 mL) mixed spices*
> 2 cups (500 mL) chicken stock (approximate)
> Pastry for double-crust, 9-inch (23 cm) pie
>   (recipe p. 15)

*Ground cloves, nutmeg, cinnamon, and allspice.

Cut chicken, beef, and pork into 1-inch (2.5 cm) cubes
and place in a large bowl. Combine with onions; cover
and refrigerate for at least 12 hours or overnight.

Layer salt pork evenly in bottom of a 3-quart (3 L)
casserole, preferably cast-iron with a cover. Layer with ⅓ of
the meat mixture and ⅓ of the potatoes; season with salt,
pepper, and spices. On a lightly floured board, roll out half
of the pastry slightly thicker than for a normal pie and
arrange on the potato layer, cutting a small round hole in

the centre. Repeat with 2 more layers of meat and potatoes seasoned with salt, pepper, and spices. Cover with the remaining pastry, again cutting a small round hole in the centre.

Slowly add enough chicken stock through the hole in the pastry until liquid appears. Cover dish and bake in a preheated 400°F (200°C) oven for 45 minutes or until liquid simmers. Reduce temperature to 250°F (120°C) and continue to bake, covered, for 5 to 6 hours more or until top crust is a rich golden brown.

Eight to ten servings

TIP: The meats may be combined with the onions and marinated in refrigerator for 24 hours.

little Anglican church, St. Bartholomew's, includes a chair that belonged to parishioner Sir John A. Macdonald. The Musée du Bas-Saint-Laurent is a lively contemporary art museum. Cacouna, with its main street of one-time English country houses, is home to woodworker Desiré Pelletier, who decorates his lawn with miniature houses and a church, all modelled on local landmarks. Take a break at Ali-Baba Crème Glacée Maison for a big choice of homemade Italian-style ice creams and sorbets. It's just east of Cacouna. Rimouski's Musée Régional, housed in an old stone church, has fine regional exhibits. Maison Lamontagne in Rimouski-Est dates from about 1750. At the lighthouse at Pointe-au-Père, a national historic site, is a museum devoted to the 1914 sinking of the *Empress of Ireland.* The loss of 1,012 lives makes it Canada's worst maritime disaster.

BLANCS DE VOLAILLES FARCIS AUX PLEUROTES ET AU FROMAGE

Chicken breasts stuffed with oyster mushrooms and cheese

Pascal Gagnon, chef at Manoir de Tilly, an inn that flourishes in a 1786 manor house in the quiet village of Saint-Antoine-de-Tilly, west of Lévis, likes to flavour his cuisine with mushrooms and cheese.

3 tablespoons (45 mL) unsalted butter
4 small shallots, finely chopped
10 ounces (300 g) fresh oyster mushrooms,
   ends trimmed
4 boneless, skinless chicken breasts
6 ounces (150 g) soft ripened cheese (such as
   triple-crème Saint-André)
2 tablespoons (30 mL) vegetable oil
½ cup (125 mL) dry white wine
1 cup (250 mL) whipping cream
2 tablespoons (30 mL) chopped fresh tarragon
Salt and freshly ground pepper

In a large, heavy, ovenproof frying pan, heat 1 tablespoon (15 mL) of the butter over medium heat and cook shallots and mushrooms, stirring, for 5 minutes, until the mushrooms release their liquid and start to brown. Transfer to a bowl. Using a sharp knife, slice each chicken breast along one side until almost cut in two. Stuff breasts with mushroom mixture and cheese, pinching edges of each breast to seal.

Add remaining 2 tablespoons (30 mL) butter and oil to frying pan over medium heat and heat until sizzling hot.

Brown chicken breasts about 5 minutes per side. Place frying pan in preheated 400°F (200°C) oven. Roast for about 7 minutes or until chicken juices run clear when meat is pierced with a fork. Transfer chicken to a platter, cover, and keep warm.

Discard pan juices. Place frying pan over medium-high heat, add wine, and stir until reduced by half. Stir in cream and cook until sauce is thick enough to coat a spoon. Add tarragon and season with salt and pepper to taste. To serve, cut each chicken breast into 3 or 4 diagonal slices, drizzle with sauce, and then serve.

Four servings

CHIARD DE GOÉLETTE

Public Gardens

Lavish gardens surround several historic houses along the south shore of the St. Lawrence River. The biggest and best-known are the Reford Gardens (Jardins de Métis), started in 1926 by Elsie Meighen Reford around a fishing lodge built at the mouth of the Mitis River by her uncle, Canadian Pacific Railway president George Stephen, later Lord Mount Stephen. Now a national historic site, the gardens at Grand-Métis attract more than 100,000 visitors a year between June and mid-October. You can visit the former Reford house, originally called Estevan and now home to a museum, restaurant, and gift shop. Call (418) 775-2222, or visit the website at www.refordgardens.com.

Fishermen's hash

This comfortable supper dish was invented by fishermen's wives for their husbands to take out in the "goélette," or fishing boat. This recipe belongs to Marie-Jeanne Levesque of Saint-Jean-Port-Joli, who recommends that the dish be served with her "biscuits matelots" (fishermen's biscuits). The secret to a good chiard, says Mme Levesque, is salt pork with a pink colour. If the meat has a greyish cast, it has lost moisture and will not give the best flavour. If you wish to reduce the salt in the meat, soak it overnight in cold water or blanch in boiling water for 5 minutes, then drain. Fat can be reduced by frying the sliced pork first, then discarding the fat drippings.

> 8 cups (2 L) peeled potatoes, cut in ½-inch
>   (1 cm) slices
> ½ pound (250 g) salt pork, finely chopped
> 1 cup (250 mL) chopped onions
> Freshly ground pepper
> Fishermen's Biscuits (recipe follows)

In a 2-quart (2 L) flameproof casserole dish, layer ⅓ each of the potatoes, salt pork, and onions; season with pepper. Continue layering ingredients two more times. Add enough cold water until almost level with top layer.

Heat mixture over medium heat, almost to boiling point; reduce heat and slowly simmer, uncovered, until potatoes are cooked and liquid has reduced, about 30 to 40 minutes. Serve with Fishermen's Biscuits, if desired. Arrange the biscuits on the surface of the casserole and partially cover for the final 10 minutes of cooking so that biscuits become moist.

Six servings

Fishermen's Biscuits

2 cups (500 mL) all-purpose flour
3½ teaspoons (17 mL) baking powder
½ teaspoon (2 mL) baking soda
½ teaspoon (2 mL) salt
2 tablespoons (30 mL) butter, shortening, or lard
¾ cup (175 mL) ice water

In a large bowl, combine flour, baking powder, baking soda, and salt. Using a pastry blender or 2 knives, cut in butter until mixture resembles coarse crumbs. Using a fork, stir in just enough water until dough will form a ball. Wrap and chill for 30 minutes.

On a lightly floured surface, roll out dough to a thickness slightly less than ¾ inch (2 cm). Use a 2-inch (5 cm) cookie cutter or glass and cut into rounds. Arrange on a greased baking sheet. Prick biscuits all over with a fork. Bake in a preheated 375°F (190°C) oven for 15 to 20 minutes or until firm and very lightly coloured.

Makes about 2 dozen

TIP: Fishermen's biscuits may be made a day ahead and stored in a closely covered container.

Another unusual garden near Sainte-Croix, west of Lévis, is the Domaine Joly-de-Lotbinière, a 19th century seigneury. The garden includes blue potato plants; after their blue flowers fade, the potatoes are made into a delicious blue potato salad served at the garden restaurant. Gingerbread trim on the 1851 manor house includes cutouts of maple leaves, but the property made horticultural history with its groves of rare black walnut trees. The garden, designed with historic themes, has a spectacular site on a bluff overlooking the river. It's open mid-June to Labour Day; call (418) 926-2462. Farther down-river, at Saint-Pacôme, is an English perennial garden that winds the length of the spacious estate of one-time lumber baron Sydney King, on the banks of Rivière Ouelle. Called Domaine des Fleurs, it specializes in lupins and other perennials. In the stables of the 1903 house are exhibits about local forestry and a before-and-after history of the gardens. It's open from June 23 to Labour Day; call (418) 852-3409.

PÉTONCLES
DES ÎLES-DE-LA-MADELEINE

Scallops with oriental seasonings

Richard Duchesneau, chef at Auberge du Mange Grenouille, the charming, red-painted Victorian inn overlooking the St. Lawrence in Bic, likes to give an oriental touch to his cuisine. This recipe for Atlantic scallops includes a ginger-flavoured mushroom sauce.

1 stalk lemongrass, white part, minced*
2 shallots, minced
1 clove garlic, minced
1¼ cups (300 mL) chicken stock
6 stalks fresh coriander
¼ cup (60 mL) extra-virgin olive oil
Salt and freshly ground pepper
1¼ pounds (625 g) large fresh scallops, trimmed,
   rinsed, patted dry
½ cup (125 mL) sesame seeds
2 tablespoons (30 mL) peanut oil
4 ounces (125 g) bean thread noodles
Mushroom Sauce (recipe follows)
Fresh coriander for trim

*Lemongrass may be replaced with ½ teaspoon (2 mL) grated lemon rind and 1 tablespoon (15 mL) chopped parsley.

Soak lemongrass in cold water for an hour; drain. Using a medium saucepan, combine lemongrass, shallots, garlic, and chicken stock. Bring to a boil and simmer until liquid is reduced to about ⅔ cup (150 mL). Cool. Add the coriander and blend in a food processor or blender until smooth. Add oil in a steady stream while motor is running, blending until smooth. Season with salt and pepper and set aside.

Roll scallops in sesame seeds, coating all sides. In a large, heavy, non-stick frying pan, heat the peanut oil over high heat until hot. Add scallops and cook until golden on both sides, just until opaque. Transfer scallops to a warm platter and keep warm.

Place the noodles in a bowl and pour boiling water over them; let stand 3 minutes, then drain and keep warm.

To serve, pour a little of the coriander sauce onto 4 warm serving plates. Arrange scallops on the sauce and turn in the sauce to coat lightly. Set oriental noodles on the side of each plate and top with mushroom sauce. Add seasonal vegetables and trim with fresh coriander.

Four servings

TIP: Both the coriander and mushroom sauces may be prepared several hours in advance. Reheat the mushroom sauce before serving.

Mushroom Sauce

2 tablespoons (30 mL) unsalted butter
12 medium white mushrooms, minced
1 green onion, chopped
1 clove garlic, chopped
½ teaspoon (2 mL) freshly grated gingerroot
1 tablespoon (15 mL) soy sauce
1 tablespoon (15 mL) rice vinegar
Pinch granulated sugar

Heat butter in large, heavy saucepan and cook mushrooms, green onion, and garlic just until the mushrooms release their liquid. Add gingerroot, soy sauce, vinegar, and sugar, stirring to blend. Keep warm.

LE PHYLLO COUREUR DES BOIS

Cheese packets with salad

A Coast of Bakeries

Travellers have a choice of bakeries and pastry shops, new and old, as they travel this coast, beginning with the handsome, 1867 seigneurial mill at Beaumont, still grinding grain on the stone. To the east is the little Boulangerie La Levée du Jour at Saint-Vallier and Boulangerie Niemand at Kamouraska. This European-style organic bakery operates in a 1903 Queen Anne revival clapboard house. Specialties are heavy whole grain loaves and fruit strudels. A lunch and tea café with a terrace is nearby, serving the bread. At Saint-Roch-des-Aulnaies, an 1842 seigneurial mill operates next to the old manor house and traditional loaves are sold in the mill's little shop. Superb cakes and gifts are

Pascal Gagnon, chef at Manoir de Tilly, likes to cook with the gouda cheese made by Fromagerie Bergeron in his village of Saint-Antoine-de-Tilly. The cheese maker seasons one of his gouda-type cheeses with cumin and names it for the fur traders of early Quebec. This recipe makes a lunch or supper dish.

> 8 sheets phyllo pastry
> ⅓ cup (75 mL) melted butter
> 7 ounces (200 g) cumin-flavoured gouda cheese Coureur des Bois*, cut in 4 pieces
> 4 thin slices prosciutto ham
> ¼ cup (60 mL) white wine vinegar
> ½ cup (125 mL) extra-virgin olive oil
> ¼ cup (60 mL) chopped fresh chives
> Salt and freshly ground pepper
> 1 can (14 ounces/398 mL) hearts of palm, drained, sliced
> 4 cups (1 L) mixed salad greens

*Substitute plain gouda cheese sprinkled with a little cumin. If larger servings are desired, double the amount of cheese and increase baking time to 10 minutes.

Arrange 1 sheet phyllo pastry on a work surface and brush with butter. Layer another sheet on top, brushing with butter. Repeat until you have 4 stacks of 2 pastry sheets each. Roll each piece of cheese in a slice of prosciutto ham, then set on edge of pastry and roll up, tucking in ends so you have a neat little package. Repeat so you have 4 pastry packages. Arrange on buttered or parchment-lined baking sheet and brush pastry with melted butter.

offered at Aux Petits Caprices, just west of Saint-Simon. Chocolate and raspberries are favourite flavours. Unusual teapots are displayed, and tea and sweet treats may be enjoyed next to a lush perennial garden. At Bic, Folles Farines is worth a major detour for its delectable French loaves, made with organic flour and long fermentation. Nearing the Gaspé, a modest bakery called La Miche Canadienne, west of Sainte-Flavie, makes a sustaining multigrain loaf.

In a bowl, combine the vinegar, oil, chives, salt, and pepper. Add the sliced hearts of palm and let stand for 1 hour.

Bake pastry packages in preheated 400°F (200°C) oven for about 7 to 9 minutes, or just until puffed and golden brown. Arrange salad greens on 4 serving plates. Top with dressing and sliced hearts of palm. Place a hot, baked pastry package on the centre of each salad.

Four servings

TIP: Pastry packages may be prepared, then covered and refrigerated for up to 4 days; bring to room temperature before baking.

LONGE D'AGNEAU AUX HERBES FRAÎCHES

Loin of lamb with fresh herbs

Claude Cyr includes local lamb and game birds on the menu of his restaurant, Au Coin de la Baie, in Métis-sur-Mer. Although the growing season is short on this stretch of the St. Lawrence, he grows plenty of herbs for his cuisine.

> 2 boneless loins of lamb, 8 ounces (250 g) each
> 1 tablespoon (15 mL) butter
> 1½ cups (375 mL) red wine
> 1 cup (250 mL) veal stock or consommé
> 1 teaspoon (5 mL) chopped fresh chives
> 1 teaspoon (5 mL) chopped fresh tarragon
> 1 teaspoon (5 mL) chopped fresh savory
> Salt and freshly ground pepper

Heat a large, heavy frying pan on medium–high, add butter and sear lamb for 2 minutes per side or until browned. Transfer lamb to a shallow roasting pan. Place in preheated 450°F (230°C) oven for 12 minutes or until medium-rare. Meanwhile, add wine to frying pan and cook until reduced to about ¾ cup (175 mL). Add the veal stock and simmer for 10 minutes or until reduced to about ½ cup (125 mL). Add chives, tarragon, savory, salt, and pepper to taste. Keep sauce warm. Transfer lamb to a warm platter and let stand at room temperature for 5 minutes. Slice meat and serve with sauce and hot steamed vegetables in season.

Four servings

TARTE AU SIROP D'ÉRABLE

Rich and simple, this delectable pie recipe belongs to Rose-Aimé Dumais, who runs a maple syrup operation, Érablière Dumais, at St. Alexandre near Rivière-du-Loup.

> 1½ cups (375 mL) maple syrup
> 1 cup (250 mL) whipping cream
> ¼ cup (60 mL) cornstarch
> ¼ cup (60 mL) cold water
> 1 baked, single, 9-inch (23 cm) pie crust
>   (recipe p. 15)

In a saucepan, combine maple syrup and cream. In a bowl, blend cornstarch with water and stir into cream mixture. Place pan over medium heat and cook, stirring, until mixture comes to a boil; cook for 2 minutes or until thickened. Pour filling into baked pie shell and let cool until set.

Six to eight servings

TIP: Pie shell may be prepared a day ahead.

Côte-du-Sud Menu

La Feuillantine de chèvre (p. 22)
Goat cheese tartlets with salad greens and sun-dried tomato vinaigrette

Pétoncles des Îles-de-la Madeleine (p. 32)
Scallops with oriental seasonings and noodles
Steamed green beans

Tarte au sirop d'érable (p. 37)
Maple syrup tart

POUDING AUX POMMES ET À L'ÉRABLE

Plums Renewed

Beside a graceful, white, 1853 mansion called Maison de la Prune, east of Saint-André-de-Kamouraska, is a hillside with a microclimate in which the plums of 17th century New France are being revived. Experimenting with hundreds of varieties of this fruit, originally transplanted from Normandy by the Recollet fathers, is historian Paul-Louis Martin, a professor at the Université du Québec à Trois-Rivières, his wife, Marie de Blois, who makes thousands of jars of plum preserves each summer, and their children, who help run the house—a one-time general store—as a fruit research centre and tourist site. You can buy the preserves, including damson plum jelly and lombard plum jam, in the shop located in the house, open daily from Aug. 1 to Oct. 31, at 129 Route 132 East, (418) 493-2616. The plum centre is classified as one of Quebec's ecological museums.

Apple maple upside-down tart

This recipe is adapted from a Métis regional cookbook called *L'ordinaire* 2 by Thérèse Beaulieu-Roy, published in Mont-Joli in 1979. It's a local version of the French upside-down dessert, "Tarte Tatin," originally served by two sisters, "Les demoiselles Tatin," after they inadvertently overcooked a tart at their inn in Lamotte-Beuvron in the Loire River valley. The classic French dessert calls for browning white sugar in a frying pan, and then braising the apples in the syrup before adding the pastry.

> 4 tart, firm cooking apples, such as Cortland or Spy
> 1 tablespoon (15 mL) butter
> ¾ cup (175 mL) maple syrup
> Pastry for single–crust, 9–inch (23 cm) pie
> (recipe p. 15)

Peel, core, and cut apples into ¾-inch (2 cm) slices. In a large, cast-iron, 9-inch (23 cm) frying pan, melt butter and tilt pan to coat the bottom evenly with butter. Remove from heat. Arrange apple wedges in concentric circles in pan and pour maple syrup over.

On a lightly floured board, roll pastry into a circle slightly larger than the size of the frying pan and arrange on top of apple slices, tucking edges under. Cut steam vents in pastry.

Place over medium heat and cook until syrup bubbles vigorously, about 5 minutes. Place frying pan in a preheated 375°F (190°C) oven and bake the tart for 30 to 35 minutes or until pastry is lightly browned. Let cool for 15 minutes. Run a knife around the edge to loosen and invert tart onto serving plate. Serve either warm or at room temperature.

Six to eight servings

CRÈME AUX POMMES

This light and foamy combination of beaten egg whites and apple-sauce is sometimes called "pommes en neige" (apples in the snow). Although best made with grated maple sugar, it can be sweetened with brown sugar or granulated sugar. It takes on a luxurious look if served in tall glasses. Cookbook authors Suzette Couillard and Roseline Normand included this recipe from L'Islet-sur-Mer in their collection entitled *Les meilleurs recettes québécoises d'autrefois* (Best Quebec Recipes of Bygone Days). Use pasteurized raw egg whites found in the dairy section of supermarkets.

> 2 egg whites, at room temperature
> ½ cup (125 mL) grated maple sugar or brown or
>   granulated sugar
> 1 cup (250 mL) unsweetened applesauce, chilled
> Grated rind of 1 lemon or orange

No more than an hour before serving, place egg whites in a bowl and beat with an electric mixer until soft peaks form. Beat in sugar, a spoonful at a time, to make a stiff meringue. Gently fold in apple-sauce and grated rind until well combined. Spoon into individual dessert dishes and refrigerate until serving time.

Four to six servings

Prime Ministerial Retreat

Two of Canada's prime ministers summered at St. Patrick, now a suburb of Rivière-du-Loup—Sir John A. Macdonald and Louis St. Laurent. Macdonald's spacious 1850 house overlooking the St. Lawrence River has been restored by the preservation group called Canadian Heritage of Quebec as a B and B, and hums with summer visitors. Breakfast on the gallery means starting with innkeeper Meredith Fisher's "St. Patrick's Sunrise," a refreshing orange and cranberry juice cocktail, followed by pancakes with maple syrup and fresh berries. Whales perform off-shore, and there's croquet, north-ern lights, and walks to admire the old riverside houses of English-speaking summer residents. The house, called Les Rochers (photo left), is at 336 Fraser St. (highway 132), St. Patrice de Rivière-du-Loup, (418) 868-1435.

CHARLEVOIX

Talk to the residents of Charlevoix and you soon hear about unusual gardens, private flower gardens of affluent summer residents, and bigger market gardens that grow exceptional foods. Tucked into hollows between the St. Lawrence River shore and distant, blue-grey mountains, flourishing despite long winters of deep snow, are microclimates—warm, verdant areas for growing giant flowers and unusual fruits and vegetables.

In the hills above La Malbaie (formerly Murray Bay) is La Ferme des Monts in Sainte-Agnès, an organic garden run by Marc Bérubé, ex-Montrealer and one-time lumberman. Down on a flat and fertile plain below Les Eboulements are two big gardens, one designed for chefs called La Métarie du Plateau. It's a second career for Jean Leblond, a one-time Quebec City television producer, who bought a farm in Charlevoix and started growing offbeat vegetables for such local chefs as Guy Bessone and Régis Hervé. He supplies restaurants as far away as the Saguenay-Lac Saint-Jean area, Tadoussac and Baie Comeau, and Quebec City. Next to Leblond's land is the Pilote family market garden, Les Jardins du Centre. It's open to the public to tour, attend tastings, and shop.

Marc Bérubé remembers arriving in the kitchen of Pointe-au-Pic chef Eric Bertrand some years ago with his organic carrots and rutabaga. "The chef said, 'These are good, but why don't you grow some baby vegetables and edible flowers?' So I did," said the grower, kneeling in the earth to pull up one of Bertrand's favourites—a "winter" radish with a pink interior. "You store it like a potato," said Bérubé. Other offbeat crops are bronze fennel, Welsh and Egyptian onions, yellow and white beets, twist-neck garlic, edible bee balm flowers, pansies, and stella dora day lilies, "the most flavourful, sweetest flower I know."

Constantly experimenting, he's now embarked on a project, as he put it, "to domesticate fiddleheads," transplanting the ferns from a stream into a moist part of his property. Bérubé refuses to grow foods that lack flavour, which means he's rejected both white potatoes and the fashionable blue ones, and will grow only yellow or red-fleshed potatoes.

Leblond grows blue potatoes, calling them a Peruvian ancestor of the white potato. "Let them cool after cooking in water to stabilize the blue colour, then make them into thin, thin fried chips," he suggests. He also recommends blue mashed potatoes. He works closely with chefs, planting seeds they bring him from Europe and often telling the chefs how best to cook his foods. His recent successes include banana potatoes and Jerusalem artichokes. Like other chefs, Régis Hervé picks his own foods at Leblond's garden. Another venture in chef-producer cooperation is Hervé's new "table champêtre" (farm restaurant) at the big lamb farm, La Ferme Eboulmontaise in Les Eboulements. Not surprisingly, lamb has the starring role on his menu.

There's a salty scent to the air and good fish to eat in this region. Trout fishing in the streams that tumble down to the St. Lawrence has replaced the salmon fishing of more plentiful times. My mother, whose family came from Toronto to summer in Pointe-au-Pic in the years before the First World War, remembered her brothers catching speckled trout, "the real delicacy of the summer, just fried in butter or lard, nothing fancy." Two tiny fish—smelt and capelin—have been caught in the river since earliest times. Fishermen used to sell strings of little smelts door-to-door. "You'd see the children on the wharf with their bamboo fishing rods," Mother remembered. "The smelts would be fresh from the cold St. Lawrence. Dipped in flour and fried, they were delicious."

The original French cuisine of local families has both British and American accents. The Scots, arriving after the British conquest, grew oats and potatoes. The English-speaking summer people from Montreal and Toronto imported their liking for cream in cooking and the steamed pudding. And the Americans introduced cornbread and Johnny cakes. Berries, picked wild on the hillsides, have always been the favourite dessert—strawberries, raspberries, or blueberries, topped only with thick cream and a sprinkling of maple sugar.

CROUSTILLANT DE TRUITE FUMÉE AU MIGNERON

Smoked trout in pastry

A Savoury Route

A guide to local food producers who sell to the public is the brainchild of the progressive chefs of the Charlevoix region. Pick up a copy of La route des saveurs de Charlevoix at tourist offices and follow the map to your choice of about 16 addresses from Baie-Saint-Paul to Cap-à-l'Aigle. At each stop, you can tour the place, then buy lamb, veal, boar, venison, fish, stone-ground flour, local cheeses, bread, fruit, or vegetables. Some restaurants serving the products are included. Participants are identified by the logo depicting a chef's toque.

Chef Dominique Truchon enjoys cooking with the Baie-Saint-Paul cheese Le Migneron. In this appetizer from his menu at Auberge des Peupliers in Cap-à-l'Aigle, he combines the cheese with smoked trout in hot, crisp pastry sacks, then adds a lively dressing.

⅓ cup (75 mL) unsalted butter, clarified*
1 leek, white part only, sliced thinly
4 sheets phyllo pastry
4 ounces (125 g) smoked trout, cut in 4 pieces
2 ounces (50 g) Migneron or Oka classic cheese,
  cut in 4 slices
⅓ cup (75 mL) extra–virgin olive oil
2 tablespoons (30 mL) finely chopped fresh chervil
2 tablespoons (30 mL) finely chopped fresh chives
¼ cup (60 mL) balsamic vinegar
Cherry tomatoes
Fresh herbs

*Heat butter gently in small saucepan until it separates; discard solids.

Heat 1 tablespoon (15 mL) of the butter in a saucepan over medium heat and cook leek for 3 minutes or until softened. Transfer to a bowl.

Place 1 sheet of phyllo pastry on work surface; brush with melted butter. Cut into 4 even–sized squares. Stack phyllo squares one on top of the other, turning a quarter turn so edges are not matching. Repeat, making 3 stacks

of squares in the same way with remaining phyllo and butter. Place a spoonful of leek in centre of each square; top with smoked trout and cheese slice. Draw up phyllo pastry around filling, twisting gently on top so that pastry edges flare out to resemble a ruffle. Set pouches on a buttered or parchment-lined baking sheet. Bake in preheated 400°F (200°C) oven for about 10 minutes, or until pastry is golden.

In a small bowl, combine oil, chervil, and chives. Place balsamic vinegar in small saucepan and boil until reduced by half. Arrange hot pastry pouches on 4 serving plates. Spoon oil and herbs onto each plate around pouches and drizzle with reduced vinegar. Decorate plates with tomatoes and herbs.

Four servings

TIP: Recipe may be prepared and set on baking sheet several hours in advance, covered closely with plastic wrap and refrigerated until ready to bake.

Time for Bread

Outdoor bread ovens built a century or more ago abound in Charlevoix, and are still being replicated today. Travel the backroads and you'll see these oval-shaped stone and cement structures with their double iron doors and roofs to contain flying sparks. Hervé Gobeil, who helped build his outdoor bread oven and uses it at his bakery called Le Temps d'un Pain! at 674 du Golf Rd., La Malbaie, says part of the reason he uses such an oven is his pride in local history. Secondly, he's convinced the movement of the hot air, circulating constantly around the bread as it bakes, turns out fine, flavourful, coarse-textured loaves with a crisp crust. Firing it up with a mixture of woods—he likes fir, spruce, and tamarack—is another key factor. He obtains stone-ground, natural flour from the Moulin Banal, the one-time seigneurial mill still operating in Les Eboulements, and mixes it half and half—white and whole wheat flours.

VELOUTÉ DE GOURGANES

Cream-topped bean soup

A Glimpse of the Past

The hillsides that rise from the St. Lawrence still show outlines of the original farms. Until the Second World War and the advent of radio changed the way we lived, artists could observe a way of life that was nearly self-sufficient. Montreal painter Jori Smith, 94, who summered from 1930 to 1970 near Petite-Rivière-Saint-François, just west of Baie-Saint-Paul, wrote about the customs in a beautiful little book *Charlevoix County, 1930.* When she and her husband, Jean Palardy, first arrived, the residents were "living exactly as in the eighteenth, seventeenth centuries, like their parents and like their grandparents...away, isolated up in the mountains." In an interview, she remembered the extreme poverty, the annual butchering of the pig, the convivial community. "It was like stepping into another age–the Middle Ages. Each family produced all its own food. They bought nothing but molasses, salt and pepper."

The "gourgane" bean, large and green with rosy streaks and seeds that resemble fava beans, was brought to New France in 1618 by Louis Hébert, the colony's first farmer-settler. It's been traced to the "fève des marais" grown around Paris. This sophisticated version of the traditional "soupe aux gourganes" is prepared by Chef Dominique Truchon of Auberge des Peupliers in Cap-à-l'Aigle. He blends it until smooth, then adds a dollop of whipped cream.

> 1 pound (500 g) fresh or frozen gourgane beans*
> 10 cups (2.5 L) chicken stock
> 1 onion, chopped
> 3 carrots, peeled, chopped
> 2 stalks celery, chopped
> ¼ pound (125 g) salt pork, in 1 piece
> 1 tablespoon (15 mL) salted herbs, homemade or
>   commercially prepared (see p. 167)
> Salt and freshly ground pepper
> Lightly whipped cream

*Substitute fresh or frozen fava beans.

Shell beans, discarding pods, and remove tiny tip of each seed, if desired. In a stockpot or large saucepan, combine beans, chicken stock, onion, carrots, celery, and salt pork. Bring to a boil, cover, and reduce heat; simmer for about 1½ to 2 hours or until beans are tender. Add salted herbs. Discard salt pork.

In a blender or food processor, purée soup in batches until very smooth; strain through a fine sieve into a

saucepan. Season with salt and pepper to taste. Heat soup
until piping hot. Ladle into bowls and add a dollop of
whipped cream, if desired.

Eight servings

TIP: Soup may be prepared several hours in advance and
then reheated.

FILETS D'ÉPERLANS À L'AIL

Garlic-fried smelts

Vacationers' Mecca

Charlevoix has long been a favourite resort for "pleasure seekers." The term was coined by my grandfather, the late University of Toronto historian George M. Wrong, in his book *A Canadian Manor and Its Seigneurs*, published in 1908. It tells the story of the Nairne seigneury in Pointe-au-Pic. Marrying into the Blake family of Toronto, who had summered in Murray Bay since the 1860s, he was able to study the family papers of Col. John Nairne, a Scots Highlander who helped Gen. James Wolfe defeat the French Canadians at the Battle of the Plains of Abraham in 1759. Nairne and fellow officer Malcolm Fraser were then granted seigneuries in Murray Bay. Fraser's property, across the Murray River at Cap à l'Aigle, has belonged to the Cabots of New England since 1902.

Fried, breaded or plain, and served with parsley, lemon, and a tartar sauce or mayonnaise, these little fish make either a first course or a whole meal in Murray Bay. This recipe is from the menu at Auberge des Peupliers in Cap-à-l'Aigle.

> 12 large smelts or 18 small smelts
> ⅓ cup (75 mL) butter
> 2 cloves garlic, chopped
> ½ cup (125 mL) fine, dry bread crumbs
> ½ cup (125 mL) freshly grated Parmesan cheese
> 2 tablespoons (30 mL) chopped fresh parsley
> Lettuce leaves
> Thinly sliced lemon

Split smelts along belly, clean, and remove backbones, fins, and tails. In a small saucepan, melt butter until bubbly and add garlic; remove from heat and strain butter into bowl. In another bowl, combine bread crumbs, cheese, and parsley. Dip smelts in garlic–flavoured butter, then dredge in bread crumb mixture. Arrange on a lightly greased baking sheet.

Bake in a preheated 425°F (220°C) oven for about 5 minutes. Transfer to a serving plate lined with lettuce leaves and sliced lemon.

Two servings

TIP: Fish may be prepared up to the point when they are to be baked, then can be covered and refrigerated. Bring to room temperature before baking.

BELLE CHASSE FORESTIÈRE

Game birds with mushroom and onion sauce

Chef Jeannot Desgagnés of Hotel la Roche Pleureuse on Île aux Coudres uses a farm-raised game bird called a "belle chasse," which is a cross between a pheasant and a guinea hen.

2 belle chasse game birds (1 pound/500 g each)
3 carrots, peeled, coarsely chopped
2 onions, coarsely chopped
4 stalks celery, chopped
Vegetable oil
½ teaspoon (2 mL) dried thyme
Salt and freshly ground pepper
2 cups (500 mL) game bird or chicken stock
1 cup (250 mL) white wine
½ cup (125 mL) chopped green onions
2 cups (500 mL) sliced mushrooms

TIP: Rock Cornish hens or pheasant may be substituted for the game birds. Birds may be prepared several hours in advance, up to the point they are roasted.

Truss by tying birds' legs and wings with string. Place carrots, onions, and celery in a large, heavy, flameproof casserole. Oil birds lightly, then season with thyme and salt and pepper to taste. Set birds on vegetables in pan. Add game bird stock to bottom of pan and roast in a preheated 350°F (180°C) oven for 1½ hours, basting occasionally with pan juices. Remove birds to hot platter and keep warm.

Strain pan juices and vegetables through a sieve into a bowl; skim off fat. Discard vegetables. Place roasting pan over high heat and add wine; cook until slightly reduced. Add strained pan juices and boil over high heat until sauce is reduced by half. Adjust seasoning with salt and pepper to taste. Add green onions and mushrooms; cook, stirring, for 3 minutes, or until softened. Pour sauce over birds and serve.

Four servings

SAUTÉ DE LAPIN TANTE IRMA

Rabbit vegetable casserole

Saga of Resort Life

Few Canadian resorts have such a scholarly or copiously illustrated history as that written by Laval University historian Philippe Dubé, author of *Charlevoix: Two Centuries at Murray Bay*. The book traces the development of the community from the 17th century French settlers through the horse-and-buggy era and the affluent 1920s to modern times. In the quarter century leading up to 1925, Charles Warren was the builder of many of the rambling summer houses, a considerable number now flourishing as comfortable inns. Architecture buffs can tour the region to see dozens of styles, surrounded by lush gardens that flourish in the pure, moist air flowing off the river. Since the 19th century, summer visitors have come from as far away as Scotland and the American mid-west. The various phases of the sprawling Manoir Richelieu, first built in 1899, are depicted in the book. In 1999, the hotel underwent a massive renovation, bringing it back to its former elegance.

One of the inns in Charlevoix where traditional cuisine is celebrated is the Hôtel la Roche Pleureuse on the eastern tip of Île aux Coudres. Opened in 1934 by the Dufour family, its menu continues to offer dishes of the late Irma and Germaine Dufour, and of Lise Dufour. Chef Jeannot Desgagnes, also an island native, prepares this Dufour family recipe for rabbit.

½ pound (250 g) salt pork, cut in thin strips
2 rabbits (2½ pounds/1.25 kg each), cut into
    8 pieces each
2 onions, coarsely chopped
¾ cup (175 mL) white wine
4 cups (1 L) veal or chicken stock
4 carrots, peeled, cut into 2 x ½ inch
    (5 x 1 cm) strips
½ teaspoon (2 mL) dried thyme
1 bay leaf
Salt and freshly ground pepper
2 cups (500 mL) whole mushrooms,
    quartered if large

Blanch salt pork in a medium saucepan of boiling water for 5 minutes; drain. In a large, heavy, flameproof casserole dish with a cover, cook salt pork over medium heat for about 7 minutes or until crisp and brown. Transfer to a large bowl.

Add rabbit pieces to casserole and cook until browned on all sides. Transfer to bowl with pork. Add onions to casserole and cook, stirring, for 5 minutes or until light golden; transfer to bowl with rabbit. Drain off fat from dish. Place over medium heat and add wine. Cook, stirring up brown bits from bottom of dish, until reduced by half.

Stir in stock, carrots, thyme, bay leaf, and salt and pepper
to taste. Stir in pork, rabbit, and onions. Cover and bake in
a 350°F (180°C) oven for 1 hour or until rabbit is tender.
Add mushrooms for the final 15 minutes of cooking time.

Eight servings

TIP: Recipe can easily be halved to serve four. The dish
may be prepared up to the point when mushrooms are
added, then refrigerated for 24 hours. Bring to room temperature and complete recipe.

TOURTIÈRE DE CHARLEVOIX

Charlevoix meat pie

Charlevoix Original

Miniature tourtières, made in the shape of turnovers and called "pâtés croches," are frequently served on Île-aux-Coudres, the island off Baie-Saint-Paul. Nowadays, the filling is usually of ground pork and onion, seasoned with ground cloves, sage, salt, and pepper; in earlier times, game meats were used. The word "croche" refers to the turnover's ropelike border, achieved by turning the sealed edge of the pastry between the fingers to give the effect of small waves.

This simple combination of meat, vegetables, and seasonings varies from region to region. In Charlevoix, the custom is to include potatoes, cut in small cubes, and sometimes to cube the meat too. This recipe belongs to Thérèse Savard, who cooked it for many years for guests at Auberge La Petite Madeleine in Port-au-Persil.

> 1 pound (500 g) stewing beef
> 1 pound (500 g) pork cut from the leg
> 2 onions, finely chopped
> Freshly ground pepper
> 4 to 5 medium potatoes, peeled, cut into ½-inch
>   (1 cm) cubes
> Salt
> Charlevoix pastry for double-crust, 9-inch (23 cm)
>   or 10-inch (25 cm) pie (recipe follows)

Cut beef and pork in ½-inch (1 cm) cubes. In casserole, combine meats, onions, and pepper to taste (do not add salt) and let stand in refrigerator for at least 1 hour or overnight.

Add potatoes to meat mixture, season with salt to taste, and add water to cover. Cover casserole and bake in a 325°F (160°C) oven for 1½ hours. (Do not allow mixture to boil or meat will be toughened and cubes of potatoes may break up.)

Remove from oven and lower temperature to 275°F (140°C). On a lightly floured board, roll out half the pastry ¼ inch (5 mm) thick and line a deep, 9-inch (23 cm) or 10-inch (25 cm) pie plate. Pour meat mixture into pastry-lined shell. Roll out remaining pastry and arrange over meat filling. Trim, crimp edges, and cut steam vents.

Return pie to oven and bake for another 1½ hours or until crust is golden.

Six to eight servings

Charlevoix Pastry

Thérèse Savard always made her tourtière with this rich pastry.

4 cups (1 L) all-purpose flour
4 teaspoons (20 mL) baking powder
¾ teaspoon (4 mL) salt
2 cups (500 g) chilled vegetable shortening
1 cup (250 mL) cold milk

In a large bowl, combine flour, baking powder, and salt. Using a pastry blender or 2 knives, cut in shortening until mixture resembles coarse crumbs. Make a well in centre of mixture and pour in cold milk. Mix gently with a fork until dough just comes together; do not overmix. Divide dough into 2 balls, cover or wrap, and refrigerate for at least 30 minutes. Makes enough for 2 double-crust, 9-inch (23 cm) pies.

TIP: Pastry may be made up to 6 hours in advance and refrigerated, covered.

GIGOT D'AGNEAU DE LA FAMILLE CADIEUX

Leg of lamb with sage

Charlevoix Menu

Velouté de gourganes (page p. 44)
Cream-topped bean soup

Gigot d'agneau de la famille
Cadieux (p. 52)
Leg of lamb with sage
Pan-browned potatoes with zucchini

Tartelettes à la crème de Chicoutai
(p.58)
*Miniature tarts with cloudberry
liqueur*

Chef Eric Bertrand uses lamb from La Ferme Eboulmontaise at his inn Auberge des 3 Canards in Pointe-au-Pic. A tireless advocate for the small, specialty food producers of his region, Eric was given the Renaud Cyr award by the Quebec agriculture department. It's named after the late Montmagny chef who first promoted using fine, local products. The large quantity of sage in this recipe mellows as the dish cooks. Steamed green beans go well with this dish.

4 cups (1 L) fresh sage leaves
4 cups (1 L) boiling water
1 cup (250 mL) pearl barley, rinsed
12 tablespoons (175 mL) extra-virgin olive oil
1 yellow pepper, cut in cubes
1 red pepper, cut in cubes
1 green pepper, cut in cubes
1 leg of lamb (6 pounds/3 kg)
4 to 6 cloves garlic, sliced
1 tablespoon (15 mL) butter
2 shallots, finely chopped
1 cup (250 mL) white wine
2 tablespoons (30 mL) old-style grainy mustard
3 tablespoons (45 mL) white wine vinegar
Salt and freshly ground pepper

Place 2 cups (500 mL) of the sage leaves in the boiling water and let stand for 20 minutes. Strain sage through a sieve set over a bowl, pressing sage with the back of a spoon. Set sage infusion aside to use in making sauce; discard limp sage leaves.

Bring a large pot of salted water to a boil, add barley, and simmer for 25 minutes, just until tender. Drain and set aside. In a large, heavy frying pan, heat 3 tablespoons (45 mL) of the oil over medium-high heat and cook the yellow, red, and green peppers, stirring, for 3 minutes. Slice 1 cup (250 mL) of the fresh sage leaves into thin strips, add to peppers in pan, and cook 1 to 2 minutes; stir in the barley. Cover and keep warm.

Make incisions all over lamb with a sharp knife and insert slivers of garlic. Brush with 3 tablespoons (45 mL) of the oil and roast in preheated 450°F (230°C) oven for 35 to 40 minutes for medium-rare. Remove meat to a hot platter and keep warm. Discard fat in pan. Place over medium heat, add butter, and cook shallots for 2 minutes or until soft; add white wine and simmer, scraping up brown bits from bottom of pan, for 3 minutes. Add mustard, vinegar, remaining 1 cup (250 mL) fresh sage, sage infusion, and salt and pepper to taste. Transfer to a saucepan, bring to a boil and simmer until reduced to 1½ cups (375 mL). Strain sauce through a sieve and place in a blender. Purée until smooth, then beat in the remaining oil in a fine stream until combined. Cut lamb into slices and serve with pepper-barley mixture and sage sauce.

Eight servings

TIP: Several hours in advance, the sage infusion may be made, the barley may be cooked, and the peppers and sage mixture prepared and combined with the barley. Also, the garlic may be inserted into the lamb.

CÔTE DE VEAU DE CHARLEVOIX
À LA CRÈME DE MORILLE

Veal chops with mushroom sauce

Chef Dominique Truchon uses local veal to make this roast, which he serves at Auberge des Peupliers with a sauce flavoured with the aperitif Pineau des Charentes.

>1 rib roast of veal (6 pounds/3 kg)
>3 tablespoons (45 mL) butter
>2 tablespoons (30 mL) vegetable oil
>3 tablespoons (45 mL) Dijon mustard
>1 teaspoon (5 mL) mixed steak spices*
>2 onions, sliced
>1¼ cups (300 mL) white wine
>Mushroom Sauce (recipe follows)

*Available in seasonings section of most supermarkets

In a large roasting pan, heat butter and oil over medium-high heat; brown veal on all sides. Transfer to a platter; brush meat with mustard and sprinkle with spice mixture. Add onions to pan and cook for 3 minutes or until softened. Add white wine; return veal to pan. Roast in preheated 400°F (200°C) oven for 15 minutes. Reduce temperature to 350°F (180°C) and continue to roast for 1½ hours for medium-rare. (Total roasting time should be about 20 minutes per pound.) Let stand for 10 minutes. Cut veal into thin slices and serve with Mushroom Sauce and fresh steamed vegetables.

Eight servings

Mushroom Sauce

1 ounce (25 g) dried morel mushrooms
1½ cups (375 mL) lukewarm water
1 tablespoon (15 mL) butter
1 large shallot, finely chopped
⅔ cup (150 mL) Pineau des Charentes*
2 cups (500 mL) veal stock or consommé
2 tablespoons (30 mL) each butter and
  all-purpose flour ("beurre manié")
½ cup (125 mL) whipping cream

*Brandy-fortified wine; may be replaced with
Madeira or dry white port.

 In a saucepan, soak mushrooms in lukewarm
water for 30 minutes. Bring to a boil and simmer
for 3 minutes. Strain through a cheesecloth-lined
sieve into a bowl; reserve soaking liquid.
 In a saucepan, heat butter over medium heat and
cook shallot stirring, for 2 minutes, or until softened. Add Pineau des Charentes and cook over
medium-high heat until reduced to ¼ cup (60 mL).
Add mushroom soaking liquid and reduce over
high heat to ¼ cup (60 mL). Add veal stock, bring
to a boil, and whisk in beurre manié until sauce is
slightly thickened. Simmer, stirring, for 3 to 4
minutes. Add cream and mushrooms, and bring to
a boil, stirring. Serve hot.

the St. Lawrence River; 181
Richelieu St., Pointe-au-Pic; expensive; casino, golf; (418) 665-3703,
(800) 441-1414; www.cphotels.ca.

Most inns do not serve lunch. Le
Passe-Temps, a restaurant run by
Jacques and Marthe Lemire, who is
the chef, specializes in exceptional
crêpes and salads; 34 Bellevue
Blvd., Pointe-au-Pic;
(418) 665-7660.

TIP: Mushroom sauce may
be made up to four hours in
advance and then reheated
gently.

CHAUSSONS AUX POMMES

Apple dumplings

This early Quebec recipe can be traced to Normandy, home of many of the province's first settlers. It's sometimes named "pommes en cage" because the fruit is baked whole in a container of pastry. Norman chefs call it "bourdelots" and use puff pastry. This recipe belongs to Rita Dufour Laurin, for many years owner-manager of Hotel la Roche Pleureuse on Île aux Coudres.

Juice of 1 lemon
6 cooking apples such as Cortland or
   Golden Delicious, peeled, cored
½ cup (125 mL) brown sugar
Cinnamon
Pastry for double-crust, 9-inch (23 cm) pie
   (recipe p. 15), or 7 ounces (200 g) puff pastry
1 egg, beaten
Maple syrup
Whipped cream (optional)

Drizzle lemon juice over prepared apples. Pack brown sugar into apple centres and sprinkle with cinnamon. On a lightly floured board, roll pastry into a rectangle, 14 x 21 inches (35 x 53 cm), and cut into six 7-inch (18 cm) squares.

Place an apple in the centre of each pastry square and moisten the 4 corners of the pastry with water. Lift up and join the corners of pastry together to enclose each apple completely. Pinch edges to seal and twist pastry at the top. Brush pastry with beaten egg. Place in a greased, shallow baking pan. Bake apples in a preheated 400°F (200°C) oven for 30 to 35 minutes or until pastry is crisp and lightly browned. Serve warm with maple syrup and whipped cream, if desired.

Six servings

ASSIETTE DE POMMES AU MIEL ET AMANDES

Apples with honey and almonds

Chef Eric Bertrand serves this easy apple dessert at Auberge des 3 Canards in Pointe-au-Pic.

3 tablespoons (45 mL) butter
⅓ cup (75 mL) granulated sugar
¼ cup (60 mL) honey
Juice of 2 medium lemons
6 cooking apples, such as Cortland, peeled, cored, cut in quarters
1 cup (250 mL/135 g) lightly toasted slivered almonds
¾ cup (175 mL) whipping cream

In a saucepan, combine butter, sugar, honey, lemon juice and apples. Bring to a boil and reduce heat to low. Cover and cook for 8 to 10 minutes or until apples are just tender. Transfer apples to 4 warmed serving plates and sprinkle with almonds. Boil poaching syrup over medium heat until it reduces and becomes syrupy. Add cream and bring to a boil. Cook until sauce is slightly thickened. Pour hot sauce over apples and serve at once.

Four servings

TARTELETTES À LA CRÈME DE CHICOUTAI

Miniature tarts with cloudberry liqueur

Chef Glenn Forbes runs the Baie-Comeau restaurant La Cache d'Amélie, rated the finest on the lower north shore of the St. Lawrence River. The liqueur Chicoutai is made from cloudberries, harvested wild in this region. It's one of a group of Quebec-made liqueurs sold in Société des Alcools du Québec stores.

Pastry

2 cups (500 mL) all-purpose flour
⅔ cup (150 mL) granulated sugar
½ cup (125 mL) chilled butter, cut in pieces
1 egg
1 teaspoon (5 mL) vanilla extract

Place flour, sugar, and butter in a food processor. Blend, using on–off turns to make coarse crumbs. In a small bowl, beat egg with vanilla. Add egg mixture to flour mixture and let machine run just until dough forms a ball. Transfer dough to a plastic bag and refrigerate for 1 hour or overnight.

Divide dough into 8 equal pieces. On a lightly floured board, roll each piece into a 3½-inch (9 cm) circle. Line large muffin cups with aluminum foil and fit dough circles into each cup. Add dried beans so pastry cups hold their shape while baking. Position oven rack in lower part of oven and preheat to 375°F (190°C). Bake pastries for about 6 minutes or until set. Remove from oven, remove beans, and prick pastry with a fork. Return pastry to oven for another 10 minutes or until crisp and just beginning to turn golden. Carefully remove pastry shells from pan; remove foil and let cool on racks. Shells will firm when cool.

Not to Be Missed

Baie-Saint-Paul has a fine Centre d'Exposition on the main street, and you may find original art in the many commercial galleries. North of town, on Monsignor de Laval Blvd., is the cheese-making interpretation centre Economusée du Fromage, run by Laiterie Charlevoix, where you can buy local cheeses, including the celebrated Migneron, made by gifted cheese maker Maurice Dufour. At Saint-Joseph-de-la-Rive is the paper-making museum Papeterie Saint-Gilles. Take the ferry from Saint-Joseph-de-la-Rive to Île aux Coudres, named for its hazelnuts by explorer Jacques Cartier in 1535, and tour the island, stopping to visit old stone windmills, one turned into a flour interpretation centre. At Les Eboulements is the Moulin Banal, built in 1790. You can tour the mill and buy stone-ground flour. Les Ateliers DeBlois on highway 362 near Sainte-Irénée sells interesting pottery and wool-knit striped socks called Bas de Julie. The traditional Murray Bay weaving and knitting is

Filling

2 cups (500 mL) light (10%) cream
½ cup (125 mL) granulated sugar
6 egg yolks
⅔ cup (150 mL) all-purpose flour
Pinch salt
2 tablespoons (30 mL) unsalted butter
3 tablespoons (45 mL) Chicoutai liqueur*
¼ to ⅓ cup (60 to 75 mL) apricot jelly
1½ cups (375 mL) blackberries, raspberries,
  blueberries, quartered strawberries, drained
  clementine sections, sliced bananas

*Substitute Cointreau, Cognac, or rum.

In a saucepan, heat cream over medium heat just until pip-ing hot; do not let boil. In a bowl, using an electric mixer, beat sugar and egg yolks until foamy and pale-coloured. Beat in flour and salt, then pour in hot cream in a stream, beating constantly. Return mixture to saucepan, set over medium heat, and whisk constantly until mixture comes to a boil. Reduce heat to low and continue to cook, whisk-ing, for 2 to 3 minutes, or until thickened and smooth. Stir in butter and liqueur. Remove from heat and cover surface of custard with plastic wrap. Let stand until lukewarm.

In a small saucepan, melt apricot jelly. Place fruit in a bowl, add jelly and stir gently to coat fruit. Just before serving, fill tart shells with custard and top with fruit. Serve immediately.

Eight servings

sold at La Quenouille on Principale St. in Pointe-au-Pic; the street is one way going east, just east of the entrance to the Manoir Richelieu and casino. The Musée de Charlevoix and the old Protestant church are on the shore. Crossing the Murray River, go north to see the Fraser Falls, then south and through Cap-à-l'Aigle to Port-au-Persil, a rocky harbour with a little 1897 Presbyterian church on the shore. The Poterie de Port-au-Persil on highway 138 displays the work of a number of potters. Cross the Saguenay River on a free ferry and tour Tadoussac, a replica of a 1600 trading post, a tiny 1747 chapel, a maritime exposition in the Maison Molson-Beattie, the Marine Mammal Interpretation Centre, and the exceptional local crafts shop Boutique Nima on the street above Hôtel Tadoussac.

TIP: Tart shells may be made the day before and stored in a closely covered container at room temperature. Custard may be refrigerated overnight; bring to room temperature before adding to tart shells.

MONTÉRÉGIE

In barns near the Ontario border at Saint-Clet, pale yellow ovals of food grow lushly in a damp darkness, shepherded by French-born endive producer Jean-Michel Schryve. Suzanne Paré Leclerc, Quebec's renowned food promoter, still remembers the day when Schryve arrived at her desk with a crate of his first crop, each of the creamy spears wrapped in protective paper. "He asked me to help sell his food and I did, and look at his endive now," she said of the vegetable that's been a basic on produce counters all over eastern Canada for the past two decades. Within a month of Schryve's visit to her office at the Quebec agriculture department, Suzanne had gathered the Montreal food writers for a Belgian endive lunch in Schryve's barn. We stood around in the gloom while Schryve shone a flashlight at thousands of pale tips. More light, he explained, and the shoots of this European delicacy would turn bitter. As we reporters feasted on endive leaves spread with duck pâté, an endive quiche, an endive salad, and crisp white wine from the Dunham winery L'Orpailleur, we listened to Suzanne's boss, Jean Garon, then Quebec's minister of agriculture, wax eloquent about the role specialty food producers, whatever their ancestry, could play in Quebec's fast-developing food scene.

How right that fiery politician was. The endive producer is only one of a number of growers to have brought foreign traditions to Quebec, contributing to the province's international flavour. Hidden away in his quiet herb garden in Sainte-Madeleine, Italian-born René Balatti started marketing his jars of pesto, chopped garlic, and various herbs mixed with the best olive oil, products which have become a fixture in city stores. A warehouse in Saint-Hubert across the St. Lawrence River from Montreal is lined, floor to ceiling, with platforms crowded with exotic mushrooms. The man in charge of Sam's Mushroom Products is Sam Tsoi from Hong Kong, a Chinese Canadian, who provides our stores with fresh oyster, enoki, and shiitake mushrooms. A French salad mix that has staked out a regular spot on our vegetable counters is Quebec-produced mesclun, baby salad greens grown by the Van Winden family of Dutch background, who provide

Saladexpresse, an innovative vegetable packer in Saint-Remi, with plenty of this salad for Quebec, and even more for American customers.

Small is beautiful to chefs and gastronomes, but the new Quebec has also mastered bigness in vegetable-growing. I still remember the shock one arctic January morning of stepping into the vast lettuce greenhouses of the Mirabel hydroponic lettuce producers and seeing the sun nourishing football-field-sized ponds of Boston lettuce. Now, oak-leaf lettuce is one of their successful new varieties. Tomatoes on the vine are coming up fast in the greenhouse world from Quebec's giant Savoura hydroponic company. Outdoors, at Sherrington and Saint-Remi, south of Montreal, a territory blessed with such rich, black earth that growers call it the "terre noire," or muckland, carrots are such a big and successful crop that many growers do a bustling export business. And each August, the slopes of Rougemont mountain colour up with fields of sweet and hot coloured peppers.

Geologists say that back about 13,000 years ago this vast, flat crescent of land that encircles Montreal was made fertile because it was under water, covered with what they call the Champlain Sea. No wonder the province's "you-pick" farms are so heavily concentrated in the Montérégie region. It makes for successful growing of strawberries and tomatoes, both south and north of the city. North of Montreal on the big island that is also home to the city of Laval, broccoli is the signature crop. Ringing the Montreal region are apple orchards, Oka to the northwest, Hemmingford to the southwest, and Saint-Hilaire to the east. Cider makers use European technology and win prizes for their bubbly.

Food produced without chemical help has slowly taken hold, helped by Equiterre, a league of 48 organic growers that supplies city subscribers with a weekly basket of fruit and vegetables from May to October. Elizabeth Hunter, the dedicated ecologist who runs this "community sustainable agriculture" (CSA) network, now has almost 2,400 Montreal families receiving what she calls a "box of surprises."

Game and rabbit farms, duck foie gras producers, specialty cheese makers, apple cider orchards, and micro-breweries abound throughout Montérégie. And you don't have to be a chef to be offered the best shopping. Travelling the backroads around Montreal, photographer Gordon Beck and I, while researching our annual summer series of articles for *The Gazette* on take-out picnics, have found that, increasingly, more fine food and drink are available off the beaten track. In region after region, we've come upon a type of store we venture is a Quebec original. Such an enterprise seems to start as a fresh fruit and vegetable stand, then adds good bread, a well-stocked delicatessen counter, pastry, and local delicacies. We've found these stores in communities as scattered as Beloeil, Granby, and Valleyfield. They're also a fixture in the Beauce and points east.

SOUPE À LA CITROUILLE

Pumpkin soup

At Auberge Handfield, a family inn at Saint-Marc-sur Richelieu, this soup, cooked originally by the late Irene Jeannotte Handfield, is a fall favourite.

4 cups (1 L) pumpkin, cut into 1-inch
   (2.5 cm) cubes*
3 cups (750 mL) chicken stock
2 tablespoons (30 mL) butter
2 tablespoons (30 mL) all-purpose flour
Pinch each ground nutmeg and ground cloves
Salt and freshly ground pepper
1 cup (250 mL) light (10%) cream

*Pumpkin purée may be substituted; add 2 cups (500 mL) or 1 can (19 ounces/540 mL) to chicken stock base, then proceed with recipe.

In a large saucepan, combine pumpkin and 1 cup (250 mL) of chicken stock; bring to a boil, reduce heat and simmer, covered, for 25 minutes or until very tender. Transfer to a bowl and reserve. Add butter to saucepan and melt over medium heat; stir in flour and cook, stirring, until bubbly. Add remaining chicken stock, bring to a boil, stirring, until thickened and smooth. Return cooked pumpkin, including any liquid, to pan. Purée in batches in a food processor or blender; strain soup through a sieve set over a bowl.

Return soup to saucepan and season with nutmeg, cloves, and salt and pepper to taste. Stir in cream and heat until piping hot but not boiling. Ladle into 6 warm bowls and serve.

Six servings

TIP: Soup may be made 24 hours in advance and refrigerated. Reheat gently until piping hot; do not let boil.

SOUPE AUX HUÎTRES

Oyster soup

Fish of the Past

Sturgeon as long as a rowboat is wide, and eels even longer, were popular and plentiful in the Richelieu River as recently as the 1940s. Thérèse Daigle of Saint-Hilaire can remember her grandfather, Arsène Gatien, taking her trolling on the river. "We would never return without one of these fish or some doré (walleye), perch, whitefish, or carp." The sturgeon would frighten her with its big teeth, "like a prehistoric monster," but it made a feast when it was baked with onions. Sturgeon is now so scarce in Quebec that it is usually imported. It is served smoked as an appetizer.

Her grandfather, who came from Brittany and knew eels well, would skin this snakelike fish right in the boat. Later, he'd boil it to get rid of the oil, cut it into large pieces, and roast it with onions and a dash of vinegar. Eels continue to be caught on the south shore of the lower St. Lawrence, but almost all the catch is exported to Europe.

Oysters were so plentiful in the St. Lawrence River a century ago, that this soup was a tradition at festival meals. Thérèse Daigle of Saint-Hilaire remembers her mother, the late Berthe Marcotte Gatien, serving it at the Christmas "réveillon."

¼ cup (60 mL) butter
2 cups (500 mL) fresh shucked oysters with
   their juice
3 cups (750 mL) milk
½ cup (125 mL) whipping cream
1 tablespoon (15 mL) chopped fresh parsley
Pinch paprika
Salt and freshly ground white pepper
Crackers

In a large, heavy saucepan, heat butter over medium heat; add oysters and their juice. Cook for about 3 minutes or until edges of oysters curl. Transfer to a bowl. Add milk and cream to saucepan and heat until piping hot; do not let boil. Add hot oyster mixture; season with parsley, paprika, and salt and pepper to taste. Serve at once in warmed soup bowls accompanied with crackers.

Six servings

FOIE GRAS DE PORTO ET AUX RAISINS

Duck foie gras with port and grapes

Montreal caterer Denise Cornellier, one of Quebec's top women chefs, has made fresh duck foie gras her specialty.

    ½ pound (250 g) raw duck foie gras, chilled
    1 tablespoon (15 mL) sherry vinegar
    ¼ cup (60 mL) port wine, late harvest vidal,
       or sauterne
    ¾ cup (175 mL) chicken stock
    ½ cup (125 mL) green or purple grapes, halved,
       seeded, peeled if skins are tough
    1 tablespoon (15 mL) butter
    Hot toast points

Using a sharp knife, cut into ½ inch (1 cm) thick slices. Heat a large, non-stick frying pan over high heat until very hot. Place half of the slices in frying pan and cook for about 30 seconds per side, or until seared and lightly browned; do not overcook or the fat will render out. Transfer to a plate and keep warm in the oven at its lowest setting. Drain fat into a bowl (reserve for another use) and wipe pan with paper towels; reheat over high heat until very hot. Cook remaining slices in the same way and place in warm oven. Reduce heat to medium, add vinegar to pan, then add port and cook until reduced to a glaze. Add chicken stock and simmer until it is reduced by almost half. Add grapes and cook just until warmed through. Stir in butter just until melted. Arrange foie gras on 4 warm serving plates. Spoon sauce over and serve with toast.

Four servings

GIBELOTTE DES ÎLES DE SOREL

Sorel fish stew

Not to Be Missed

Tourist attractions in the region include: the trails on Mont-Saint-Hilaire, McGill University's mountain park; the beautiful old houses and churches of Varennes and Verchères; the Centre d'interpretation du patrimoine de Sorel; the Maison nationale des Patriotes in Saint-Denis-sur-Richelieu; Fort Chambly National Historic Site in Chambly; Fort Lennox National Historic Site in Saint-Paul-de-l'Île-aux-Noix; the Canadian Railway Museum at Saint-Constant, where 130 antique railway cars and engines are on view all summer; the Musée Marsil heritage house in Saint-Lambert; the Parc historique de la Pointe-du-Moulin on Île Perrot; the Lieu historique national de Coteau-du-Lac in Coteau-du-Lac; the Musée régional de Vaudreuil-Soulanges at Vaudreuil-Dorion; the Sanctuaire Notre-Dame-de-Lourdes at Rigaud; and the recreated 18th century village, "Il était une fois…une petite colonie," at L'Acadie.

Many years ago, a small restaurant on one of the islands off Sorel began serving the day's catch of "barbotte," the plentiful little catfish from the St. Lawrence, as part of a sustaining vegetable stew. The dish was called "gibelotte," a term that France's culinary bible *Larousse gastronomique* defines as rabbit stew and traces to the Old French "gibelet," or platter of birds. The island's fish dish became popular throughout the area. Families would simmer a variety of vegetables and fish, often perch, for several hours. Sometimes they would make a convenient version of gibelotte with canned vegetables.

Today, the dish is celebrated each July at its own festival in Sorel. Montreal's Institut de tourisme et d'hôtellerie du Québec provided this recipe for the festival. Chef-researchers used a variety of fresh vegetables cooked just until tender-crisp in the stew, which is served with pan-fried fish fillets.

½ pound (250 g) salt pork
2 onions, chopped
3 cloves garlic, finely chopped
6 medium potatoes, peeled, cubed
3 cups (750 mL) chicken stock
3 cups (750 mL) beef stock
Bouquet garni*
Salt and freshly ground pepper
¼ cup (60 mL) tomato paste
2 tomatoes, peeled, seeded, diced
1 cup (250 mL) fresh, frozen, or canned
  corn kernels
1 cup (250 mL) fresh green and yellow beans,
  trimmed, cut into 1-inch (2.5 cm) lengths
½ cup (125 mL) fresh or frozen green peas
2 carrots, peeled, diced

⅓ cup (75 mL) all-purpose flour
1 teaspoon (5 mL) paprika
1 teaspoon (5 mL) dry mustard
2 pounds (1 kg) fresh perch or catfish fillets
Butter and vegetable oil for frying

*1 small stalk celery, 1 branch thyme, bay leaf, and parsley tied in a cheesecloth bag

Soak salt pork in cold water for 1 hour, then cook in boiling water for 1 hour. Drain and cut into thin strips. In a large saucepan, fry salt pork over medium heat, stirring, for 5 minutes or until crisp. Add onions and garlic; cook, stirring, for 3 minutes or until softened. Add potatoes, stock, and bouquet garni; season with salt and pepper to taste. Bring to a boil; reduce heat and simmer, covered, for 10 to 12 minutes. Stir in tomato paste, tomatoes, corn, beans, peas, and carrots. Simmer, covered, for 15 to 20 minutes or until vegetables are tender. Keep warm.

In a large, shallow bowl, combine flour, paprika, and dry mustard; season with salt and pepper to taste. Lightly coat fish fillets in seasoned flour. In a large, heavy frying pan, heat enough butter and oil to coat the bottom of the pan and fry the fillets in batches over medium-high heat until golden on both sides.

To serve, ladle the hot vegetable stew into large, heated soup bowls and serve with fried fish fillets on the side.

Six to eight servings

TIP: Soup may be made several hours in advance and refrigerated, covered. Reheat, cook the fish fillets, and serve.

SELLE D'AGNEAU RÔTIE AU GIROFLE

Clove-flavoured roast lamb

Nature's Freezer

A cold winter allowed early settlers to preserve meat outdoors. The late Jehane Benoit, a Quebec food writer and television communicator, once reminisced about the technique: "I can remember my grandfather in Saint-Isidore-de-Laprairie digging a hole in the ground big enough to hold a cauldron containing a lamb. He would wrap it in cloth and paper, add plenty of snow and some coarse salt. And the lamb would be perfectly preserved for the winter." Curious to test his system, she experimented with a lamb carcass at her farm in Sutton. "You have to dig deep, and we don't have the winters of early days. I remember my main problem was keeping enough snow piled on top. But the system worked," she said.

Chef Normand Laprise (photo opposite) of Montreal's celebrated Toqué! restaurant was one of the first Quebec chefs to serve the new pré-salé lamb from Île Verte on the lower St. Lawrence. He orders it each August and uses every part of the lamb in various ways. This roast, flavoured with cloves and herbs, is a luxury dish.

> 1 saddle of lamb, 1½ to 2 pounds (750 g to 1 kg)*
> 2 tablespoons (30 mL) olive oil
> 1 teaspoon (5 mL) chopped fresh thyme
> 1 teaspoon (5 mL) chopped fresh rosemary
> ¼ teaspoon (1 mL) ground cloves
> Salt and freshly ground pepper
> 5 tablespoons (75 mL) butter
> 1 onion, chopped
> 1 carrot, chopped
> 2 cloves garlic, chopped
> 1 small tomato, chopped
> ½ cup (125 mL) beef or chicken stock
> Cold water

*Have butcher debone lamb, keeping the flank attached to the loin, removing the tenderloin and saving the bones.

Brush bones with half of the oil and place in a shallow roasting pan. Roast in preheated 450°F (230°C) oven for 15 to 20 minutes or until well browned. Remove bones and reserve. Skim off fat. Reduce oven temperature to 400°F (200°C). Remove fat from meat, being careful not to detach the flank portion. Spread saddle of lamb on its back on cutting board and cover with a sheet of plastic wrap; pound flank portion with a meat pounder until it is very thin and large enough to wrap around the loin. Set tenderloin on flank. Sprinkle meat with thyme, rosemary, half the cloves, salt, and pepper; spread with 1 tablespoon (15 mL) of the butter. Roll flank around tenderloin and secure firmly with string. Season roast with salt, pepper, and the remaining cloves.

In a large, heavy frying pan, preferably cast-iron, heat 1 tablespoon (15 mL) butter and remaining oil over medium-high heat and brown meat on all sides for 8 to 10 minutes, turning frequently. Pour off accumulated fat. Add onion, carrot, garlic, tomato, and browned bones to pan. Roast for 12 to 15 minutes or until medium-rare; an instant-read thermometer inserted in the roast should register 135°F (60°C). Remove from oven and transfer roast to a heated platter; cover and let stand at room temperature for 15 minutes.

To make the sauce, add stock to roasting pan along with enough water to just cover the vegetables. Place over medium heat and cook for 12 to 15 minutes, stirring occasionally. Remove bones and strain mixture through a fine sieve into a bowl, pressing to extract juices. There should be 1 cup (250 mL) stock. In a small, heavy saucepan, heat remaining butter just until it begins to turn golden. Add the strained liquid and cook until reduced by half. Season with salt and pepper to taste.

To serve, remove string and cut meat into thick slices. Arrange slices on 4 warm serving plates and drizzle some of the sauce over meat. Serve the remaining sauce in a sauceboat.

Four servings

SALADE D'OIE AU CELERIRAVE

Sliced goose with celery root salad

French-born Alain Pignard, executive chef of Montreal's Queen Elizabeth Hotel, prides himself on seeking out the latest Quebec specialty food products to serve in the hotel's Beaver Club restaurant. This appetizer uses free-range goose from Baie-du-Febvre, east of Sorel. He roasts the rich-tasting meat to serve with a refreshing salad. Duck may replace the goose.

1 small celery root (celeriac), about 8 ounces
  (250 g)
Ice water
Juice of 1 lemon
⅓ cup (75 mL) mayonnaise
1 to 2 teaspoons (5 to 10 mL) maple vinegar or
  cider vinegar
2 tablespoons (30 mL) extra-virgin olive oil
1 tablespoon (15 mL) grainy mustard
2 goose or duck breasts (1 pound/500 g), skin on
2 cups (500 mL) baby salad greens or mesclun
1 ripe tomato, peeled, seeded, chopped

Several hours ahead, use a sharp knife to peel the celery root and slice it into thin, matchstick (julienne) strips. Drop immediately into a bowl of ice water mixed with the lemon juice to prevent discolouring. Drain and pat dry with towels. In a bowl, combine celery root, mayonnaise and vinegar, cover tightly, and refrigerate for up to 2 hours.

In a small bowl, whisk oil with mustard until smooth. Set aside. Using a sharp knife, cut diagonal slits into skin of goose. Heat a large, heavy frying pan, preferably cast-iron, over high heat. Place goose in pan, skin side down, and cook until well browned; turn and brown other side. Arrange meat skin side up in pan and place pan in preheated 350°F (180°C) oven; roast for 10 to 15 minutes for goose, 5 minutes for duck, or until medium-rare. Remove from oven and let meat cool to room temperature. (Reserve pan drippings for another use such as cooking potatoes.)

To serve, cut meat into thin slices. Arrange salad greens and tomatoes on 4 serving plates. Set an equal amount of the celery root salad beside the greens. Arrange sliced meat in a fan shape alongside salad and drizzle mustard sauce over meat.

Four servings

TIP: Celery root salad may be prepared and refrigerated up to 2 hours ahead. Mustard sauce may be made several hours in advance. Meat may be prepared 2 hours in advance.

Country Comes to Town

Montreal public markets date back to 1657 in Place Royale in what's now Old Montreal. Three big city markets now flourish, offering country market gardeners stalls for selling their produce in town, a custom that's been diluted in most North American cities, where markets now focus as much on crafts and restaurants as on fresh, locally grown food. Montreal's biggest market is the north-end Jean Talon Market, a multi-ethnic crossroads for fruit, vegetables, and plants. Next in size is the west-end Atwater Market, where some shoppers and vendors are English-speaking. Smallest is Maisonneuve Market in the east end. Each location operates year-round and includes among its food stores shops that sell specialty food products from all over Quebec, plus local wines, beers, and ciders.

SALADE D'AUTOMNE POMME AU MIEL TIÈDE

Salad with honey-broiled apples

Years ago, two old houses on a residential street in Saint-Bruno were made into one of this region's best restaurants, La Rabastalière. Quebec-born Chef Claude Lépine likes to serve local products in light but classic dishes. His attractive salad shows off the region's apples and honey.

> 1 medium head Boston lettuce
> A few leaves of red chicory or red-tipped
>   leaf lettuce
> 2 large endives, cored, separated into leaves
> 4 apples (Melba, Spartan, or McIntosh)
> ¼ cup (60 mL) liquid honey
> Cider Vinegar Dressing (recipe follows)

Tear Boston lettuce and chicory into bite-size pieces. Separate leaves of endives. Wash and dry salad greens and place in a bowl. Peel apples and core; slice each into 4 equal rings. Arrange on baking pan and brush with honey. Place under preheated broiler, turning once, until lightly browned.

Arrange endive leaves, pointing outward, around edges of 4 serving plates. Pour dressing over lettuce and arrange in centre of plates; top with hot apple slices. Serve immediately.

Four servings

Cider Vinegar Dressing

1 tablespoon (15 mL) cider vinegar
1 tablespoon (15 mL) apple cider
1 teaspoon (5 mL) chopped shallots
Salt and freshly ground pepper
¼ cup (60 mL) olive oil

In a bowl, combine cider vinegar, cider, and shallots. Season with salt and pepper to taste; whisk in olive oil. Pour into a jar with a tight-fitting lid and refrigerate if making ahead. Bring to room temperature and shake well before serving. Makes about ⅓ cup (75 mL).

TIP: Dressing may be refrigerated, covered, for up to 2 weeks. Lettuce may be prepared an hour in advance and refrigerated.

PAIN DE CAMPAGNE

French country bread

The Habitant

Quebec's early farmers ate mainly bread, pork, dried peas, and fresh vegetables from their garden or root cellar, in particular onions, cabbage, and squash. A meal of game or fish or eggs relieved the routine of pea soup, salt pork, and bread, according to historian Allan Greer's book, *Peasant, Lord, and Merchant: Rural Society in Three Quebec Parishes 1740-1840.* The Richelieu River valley "habitants" that Greer studied were self-sufficient, buying only salt, molasses, and rum. By the 18th century, they ate more potatoes and less bread, preferring to sell some of their wheat to generate income. Corn, beans, peas, and oats were other regular crops. Butter was a basic, but Greer found that cheese was made only after 1840.

James MacGuire, chef-owner of Le Passe-Partout, a small but renowned Montreal restaurant and bakery, is a disciple of France's bread guru, Raymond Calvel, who was awarded the French Legion of Honour for his efforts to return bakers to methods of bread-making used before mechanization. The early method, involving natural ingredients and long fermentation of the dough, gives the loaves a rich taste, chewy texture, and keeping quality for at least two days. James' recipe for this coarse, peasant bread was adapted for the home cook by Montreal baking specialist Cécile Hamel, who calls the cool water used to proof the yeast "the genius touch" because it gives the bread a long, slow rise. James and a handful of similar-minded bakers have inspired a big improvement in Quebec bread-baking in the past 10 years.

Starter

   1½ cups (375 mL/250 g) unbleached
      all-purpose flour
   ½ teaspoon (2 mL) quick–rising dry yeast
   1 teaspoon (5 mL) salt
   ¾ cup (175 mL) cool water

In a mixing bowl, combine flour, yeast, and salt; stir in water. Knead for 1 minute or until smooth. Cover with plastic wrap and a towel; set in a warm, draft–free place such as the top of the refrigerator. Let rise for at least 4 hours, or overnight, until dough has risen and bubbled up.

Dough

   1¼ to 1½ cups (300 to 375 mL/175 g) unbleached
      all-purpose flour
   ½ cup (125 mL/75 g) stone–ground whole wheat
      flour

2½ teaspoons (12 mL) quick-rising dry yeast
½ teaspoon (2 mL) salt
¾ cup (175 mL) cool water
Starter (recipe above)

In a large bowl, combine 1¼ cups (300 mL) all-purpose flour, the whole wheat flour, yeast, salt, water, and starter. Stir vigorously with wooden spoon. Add enough additional all-purpose flour to make a soft, slightly sticky dough. Place on a lightly floured board and knead for 8 to 10 minutes, or until dough is springy to the touch. Place in a lightly greased bowl and turn to grease other side. Cover and set in a warm place; let rise for 30 minutes. Turn dough over; do not punch down. Let rise for 15 to 30 minutes, or until dough keeps finger imprint. Shape into a round loaf by pulling sides under. Set on a greased baking sheet, cover, and let rise again for about 45 minutes more, or until doubled in bulk. (As this dough contains a fair amount of yeast, it is important not to let the dough rise too long before baking. It should still feel a little springy before baking to rise properly in the oven.) Bake at 400°F (200°C) for 40 to 45 minutes until golden brown and hollow-sounding when rapped with the knuckles. Makes 1 round loaf.

TIP: Starter may be made up to 3 days in advance, refrigerated, covered, then brought to room temperature before proceeding. Bread may be frozen for up to a month.

BETTERAVES MARINÉES

Pickled beets

This family recipe is regularly served at Auberge Handfield at Saint-Marc-sur-Richelieu. It dates back to the late Irene Jeannotte Handfield, who served it with tourtière or cold meats at the inn.

> 4 to 5 medium whole beets
> 2 onions, sliced
> 7 whole cloves
> 1 cup (250 mL) vinegar
> ½ cup (125 mL) water
> 5 small, dried, hot, red chilies
> 1 tablespoon (15 mL) coarse salt
> 5 whole black peppercorns
> ½ teaspoon (2 mL) dried thyme
> 1 bay leaf

Cook beets in boiling, salted water just until tender, about 40 minutes; drain, peel, and either slice or cut into cubes. Arrange layers of cooked beets and raw onion slices alternately in a 1-quart (1 L) sterilized jar along with 2 cloves.

In a saucepan, combine vinegar, water, chilies, the 5 remaining cloves, salt, peppercorns, thyme, and bay leaf. Bring to a boil; reduce heat and simmer for 5 minutes, then strain. Pour over beets and onions in jar. Seal jar, refrigerate, and let marinate for 1 month before serving.

Makes a 1-quart (1 L) jar.

Original Drinks

Quebec's micro-brewing industry offers a variety of top-rated beers and ales. But stronger stuff also bears "Made in Quebec" labels. Fruit grown off the beaten track is being made into some unique Quebec liqueurs to sell in Société des Alcools du Québec stores. One called Amour en Cage is based on ground cherries harvested south of Montreal at Saint-Athanase-d'Iberville. The most unusual is the best-seller—Chicoutai, a wild and slightly bitter drink made from cloudberries harvested on the lower north shore of the St. Lawrence River in Montagnais Indian country. Another of the six varieties is L'Orléane, a black currant liqueur created by Île d'Orléans' prize-winning wine maker Bernard Monna. Minaki has a peppery blueberry flavour. Two of these drinks contain maple syrup—one an eau-de-vie called Fine Sève, the other a rye whisky blend called Sortilège.

POMMETTES PAR LA QUEUE

Crab apples on the stem

The sour little apples from crab apple trees used to be made into this delicious dessert by the late Berthe Marcotte Gatien. "They were always the first apples of the season to ripen," her daughter, Thérèse Daigle, remembers.

> 3 cups (750 mL) water
> 3 cups (750 mL) small, early crab apples, with stems
> 2 cups (500 mL) granulated sugar

Bring water to a boil in a medium saucepan. Add apples and cook for 2 to 3 minutes or just until skins puff; do not overcook or skins will break. (Do not pierce with a fork to test for tenderness or skins will tear.) Remove, using a slotted spoon, and place on a platter.

Add sugar to water in pan and bring to a boil; cook until slightly thickened and syrupy, about 10 to 12 minutes. Return apples to syrup and cook for 2 to 3 minutes more, then remove from syrup with a slotted spoon and let cool on a platter.

Continue cooking apple syrup until it has reduced and reached gel stage. To test, dip a chilled metal spoon into boiling mixture. When 2 drops run together to form 1 large sheet that drops off the spoon, the gel stage has been reached. Cool syrup until set. Serve cooled apples with jelly, 2 or 3 per serving, as a dessert or snack.

Eight servings

TIP: Apples may be made up to five hours in advance.

PAIN À LA COMPOTE DE POMMES

Applesauce bread

At the Petch family orchard at Hemmingford, apple pies, apple doughnuts, apple butter, and apple juice are made and sold to "you-pick" apple visitors each fall. Time-honoured family recipes include this bread, which Carol Petch likes to make with a large, red, striped September apple called Wolf River. McIntosh and Cortland apples are alternatives.

½ cup (125 mL) shortening or butter, softened
1¼ cups (300 mL) packed brown sugar
2 eggs
1 cup (250 mL) thick, cold applesauce
1 cup (250 mL) raisins
1 cup (250 mL) walnuts, chopped
1¾ cups (425 mL) all–purpose flour
1 teaspoon (5 mL) baking powder
1 teaspoon (5 mL) baking soda
1 teaspoon (5 mL) each ground nutmeg and
  cinnamon
½ teaspoon (2 mL) ground allspice
½ teaspoon (2 mL) salt

The Melon Story

The orange-fleshed cantaloupe melon, dubbed a super-food by nutritionists, has been successfully grown by market gardeners in Laval, north of Montreal, since 1983 and floods city markets each August. But the more remarkable melon story concerns a musk melon of Persian origin, first grown in Montreal in 1623. Called the Montreal melon, it could grow as big as a medium pumpkin, had a heavily ribbed surface, juicy pale green flesh, and a mildly spicy flavour. Commanding high prices, the melon was demanding to grow and so delicate that when the Gorman and Décarie families of Montreal grew it about 100 years ago, they packed it in fine hay in wicker baskets to transport to such hotels as the Windsor in Montreal, Château Frontenac in Quebec City, and Waldorf Astoria in New York. The melon acquired a royal name after one was shipped to King Edward VII, causing Anatole Décarie to add the king's name to the melon on his horse-drawn delivery wagon. Gradually replaced by hardier melons, the fruit came back into

In a large bowl, cream shortening with brown sugar until fluffy. Beat in eggs until incorporated. Stir in applesauce until combined. In another bowl, combine raisins, walnuts, and ½ cup (125 mL) of the flour. In a third bowl, combine remaining flour, baking powder, baking soda, nutmeg, cinnamon, allspice, and salt.

Stir flour mixture into creamed mixture to make a smooth batter. Fold in floured raisins and walnuts. Spread batter evenly in a greased 9 x 5 inch (2 L) loaf pan.

Bake in a preheated 325°F (160°C) oven for 1¼ to 1½ hours or until a tester inserted in centre comes out clean. Cool in pan for 10 minutes, then turn out onto a rack to cool completely.

Makes 1 loaf

prominence in the 1990s, when the seeds were traced to an heirloom seed storage in Iowa and Île Perrot organic market gardener Ken Taylor (photo above) successfully grew the fruit. The next Quebec melon project might be to restart growing the Oka melon, which the Trappist monks of Oka last produced in 1973.

EASTERN TOWNSHIPS

Beautiful, tranquil, and rich in waterways and mountains, the region of Quebec southeast of Montreal has become a holiday area. Village streets have shops selling fine food, chocolates, antiques, and crafts alongside the basic grocery and hardware stores. Back roads, once lined with split-rail fences, reveal the presence of "gentlemen" farmers with their fieldstone walls or white-painted paddocks. Cattle-rearing is in fashion. Just down the road from my house in Brome county is a herd of prize-winning shorthorns. Over another hill, black Dexter cattle, pheasants, and partridges are being raised in luxury premises. The best sights for tourists are the pastures of long-horned, long-haired highland cattle, or perhaps those of red deer, boar, and ostriches. Driving south to Sutton, I always check for llamas on the golf club on the hill. These large but apparently soft-footed creatures are occasionally hired away from their nearby farm as luxury golf caddies.

Restaurants flourish in century-old clapboard houses, and specialty food producers have taken over one-time family homesteads. The region's variety of ethnic groups adds character to the townships. Evidence of their roots is plentiful—a tiny stone angel marking an old Polish cemetery outside Knowlton, a Ukrainian chapel near Vale Perkins, an annual Swiss national day party at Sutton mountain.

The food customs of the founding settlers, English and French, continue to be the basis of family cuisine. The English tradition reflects American ties with such dishes as corn or fish chowder, Boston baked beans, New England boiled dinner, brown bread, pumpkin pie, Johnny cake, and dried fruit and nuts in desserts. "Putting down" the harvest is a thriving tradition, be it in bread-and-butter pickles, mustard beans, pickled beets, or green tomato relish. At the church and fundraising suppers, out come the British links—roast beef, lamb stew, oatmeal bread, tea biscuits, scones, fruit cake, shortbread cookies, and, the centrepiece of a "strawberry social," shortcake.

The French influence has strengthened in recent years as food entrepreneurs have deserted the cities to open country stores selling the best pâtés, cheeses, and baking to affluent weekenders. Early Quebec dishes have blended into the general domaine—pea soup, pâté, tourtière, baked ham, meatball ragoût, and maple syrup pie.

The first English-speaking settlers were United Empire Loyalists, hardy New England frontier families who left the newly independent American states by the thousands, beginning in 1792, to carve farms out of the hilly terrain of the townships. Whenever I drive south into the "northeast kingdom" of Vermont, I find familiar architecture that reveals the many links between Quebec and New England. Similar styles of roofs, doorways, and gingerbread trim can be found on either side of the border.

Even before the French seigneurial system ended in 1854, French settlers came to the townships looking for their own land. The winds of language politics may blow through this multi-ethnic area, but the founding peoples have always lived side by side in a harmony that's become a model for other parts of the province.

In some areas, acceptance of sophisticated—and costly—restaurant cuisine has come slowly. With two seasons in which to make a good living—summers of watersports, golf, and tennis, winters of skiing—restaurateurs have needed the same kind of fortitude that led the first settlers to clear their land. French-born Chef Jean-Yves Prod'homme couldn't make a success of his elegant, expensive restaurant L'Aubergade in Cowansville. After two years he moved it, successfully, to the larger town of Granby in 1989. Another French chef-owner who has survived slim times is Denis Maneuge, who runs Mansonville's Boulangerie Owl's Bread, a restaurant, bakery, and delicatessen. Lately, more city people come for weekends year-round and more palates have become tuned to fine cuisine. Quebec-born Chef Pierre Johnston, who took over a small Cowansville steak and crêpe restaurant called McHaffy's in 1988 and persisted at serving his lively regional cuisine, turned the establishment into a gastronomic stop for Brome county. And one of the finest inns, Auberge Hatley in North Hatley, has inspired other restaurants around Lake Massawippi to serve fresh, regional cuisine, a persistence rewarded when the inn received the prized five-diamond rating of the Canadian and American automobile associations.

It wasn't so long ago that the only distinctive township foods were Brome Lake ducks, farm-raised trout, maple syrup, and Saint-Benoît-du-Lac cheese. Now there's a variety of game being farmed, organic and miniature vegetables grown, specialty cheeses made, wild mushrooms harvested, fine bread baked, and even garlic flowers preserved in sunflower oil and lemon juice for the flavour-seeking chefs and gastronomes. Some fine products are sold in jars—duck and pork pâté flavoured with port from Brome Lake ducks and madeira-flavoured duck or rabbit pâté from La Girondine, a duck foie gras producer in Frelighsburg. The Dunham wine region improves its products year by year and now has an ice cider made by Les Blancs Côteaux that, while no challenge to Niagara's ice wine, is livening up chefs' desserts.

Despite the new gastronomy, the festivals of the townships continue to celebrate the long-established foods—bread in Cookshire in June, dairy products in Coaticook in August, the grape harvest in Magog in September, and duck in Knowlton in October. But there's modern marketing too; the duck festival's snack, a frankfurter look-alike called the hot duck, is now available frozen year-round.

SALADE TIÈDE DE CANARD À L'ANIS ÉTOILÉ

Warm duck salad with star anise

Pierre Johnston, chef at McHaffy's, a fine little restaurant in Cowansville, likes to use duck on his menu. Barbary duck is his favourite, but with Brome Lake Ducks, the biggest duck producer in eastern Canada nearby, he uses these ducks, the Pékin variety, removing their fat and preparing the meat with lively flavourings.

> 4 boneless duck breasts, skin on, trimmed of
>   surplus fat
> ⅓ cup (75 mL) red wine
> ⅓ cup (75 mL) duck or chicken stock
> 2 star anise
> 3 cups (750 mL) mizuna greens or a mixture of
>   mesclun greens and watercress
> 4 green onions, sliced

Using a sharp knife, cut 3 small incisions in skin of each duck breast to prevent meat from curling as it cooks. Heat a large, heavy frying pan on high. Add duck breasts, skin side down, and sear for about 7 minutes, until skin is crisp and browned. Transfer duck to a plate and keep warm. Discard pan drippings; add red wine, stock, and star anise to pan. Bring to a boil, reduce heat to medium, and cook for about 5 minutes or until sauce is reduced by half. Return duck to pan, skin side up, and cook from 2 to 5 minutes, or until desired degree of doneness. Arrange greens and green onions on 4 serving plates. Slice the duck breasts on the diagonal into thin slices, arrange on greens, and drizzle both duck and salad with the warm pan juices. Serve at once.

Four servings

Eastern Townships Menu

Salade tiède de canard à l'anis étoilé (p. 83)
Warm duck salad with star anise

Omelette aux champignons sauvages (p. 88)
Wild mushroom omelette

Gâteau Reine Élisabeth (p. 96)
Queen Elizabeth cake

CHÈVRE FRAIS ET TOMATES CONFITES SALADE FOLLE DE ROQUETTE

Goat cheese with honeyed tomatoes and arugula

Artists' Potpourri

Curious to see artists and crafts-people at work in their studios, thousands of visitors travel the Townships each summer to three art shows. In mid-July is the Tour des Arts, which runs for nine days in the Sutton-Knowlton-Mansonville region. Potters, painters, weavers, and woodworkers making toys and furniture are part of this show-and-sell, started in 1988 to demonstrate the creative process. Evening concerts, literary readings, and plays are part of this celebration of the arts. For information, call (450) 242-3555 or visit www.acbm.qc.ca/tour-des-arts. A number of the participants also display their work year-round at Farfelu, their cooperative store in Sutton (for information, call [450] 538-5959). A spinoff of this tour since 1994 is the Circuit des Arts, which runs for nine days in late July in the region around Lakes Memphramagog and Massawippi.

Alain Labrie, chef at Auberge Hatley in North Hatley, makes this appetizer with goat cheese from the Chesterville cheese maker Fromagerie Tournevent. He uses a special round mould sold at kitchen equipment shops, but a round cookie cutter may be substituted. Another serving suggestion would be to spread goat cheese on toasted baguette slices. To make, brush slices with olive oil and toast in a 350°F (180°C) oven. Top each slice with basil leaf and tomato.

2 large, ripe plum tomatoes
¼ cup (60 mL) honey
1 clove garlic, chopped
Pinch cayenne pepper
7 ounces (200 g) goat cheese, cut in 12 pieces
12 small fresh basil leaves
Coarse salt
2 tablespoons (30 mL) chicken stock
2 tablespoons (30 mL) sherry vinegar
2 cups (500 mL) lightly packed fresh basil leaves
¼ cup (60 mL) extra–virgin olive oil
Salt and freshly ground pepper
6 cups (1.5 L) arugula or mixed salad greens

Remove tomato cores. Plunge in saucepan of boiling water for 15 seconds to loosen skins; transfer to cold water, drain, and peel. Cut tomatoes lengthwise into 4 pieces each. Remove seeds and inner pulp. In a small frying pan, combine tomatoes, honey, garlic, and cayenne pepper. Simmer over low heat for 3 to 5 minutes, or until tomatoes are just softened. Drain on paper towels; let cool. Meanwhile, line a round mould, 2¼ inches (5.5 cm) in diameter and 2 inches (5 cm) high with plastic wrap. Place 1 piece of cheese in bottom and spread evenly. Layer with 1 tomato piece and 2 basil leaves. Season lightly with coarse salt. Repeat layers with goat cheese, tomato piece, basil leaves, and salt. Spread top with goat cheese. Carefully remove from mould and wrap well. Repeat process to make three more cheese rounds. Refrigerate at least 2 hours or overnight.

Vinaigrette: In a blender or food processor, purée chick-en stock, sherry, and 2 cups (500 mL) packed fresh basil leaves. With machine running, pour in olive oil and blend or process until smooth. Season with salt and pepper. To serve, spread 4 salad plates with arugula or mixed salad greens. Cut each cheese round in half lengthwise and arrange in the centre of the plates. Drizzle salad and cheese with basil vinaigrette and serve immediately.

Four servings

TIP: Tomato and cheese moulds may be made up to 24 hours in advance and refrigerated, covered. Vinaigrette may be made several hours in advance and refrigerated.

Some of its artists open their studios, others join in group shows in community centres (call [819] 843-2744 or visit http://circuitdesarts.com). Then, for three weekends in late September and early October, 20 artists and craftspeople in the wine and apple region between Mystic and Frelighsburg open their studios to the public for the Tournée des 20 (call [450] 298-5630, [450] 248-7800, or [450] 295-2621, or visit www.art-t20.qc.ca).

RAGOÛT D'AGNEAU

Lamb and vegetable stew

This lamb and vegetable stew is a family recipe belonging to Constance Richard of West Brome. It was printed in a collection of traditional Townships dishes called *100 recettes d'Antan,* published in 1976 by the Cercle de Fermières de Cowansville.

> 3 to 4 pounds (1.5 to 2 kg) fresh lamb shoulder
> ¼ cup (60 mL) all-purpose flour
> ¼ cup (60 mL) bacon fat or vegetable oil
> 1 large onion, chopped
> 2 carrots, peeled and chopped
> 2 stalks celery, chopped
> 2 tablespoons (30 mL) chopped fresh parsley
> 1 teaspoon (5 mL) dried thyme
> 1 bay leaf
> Salt and freshly ground pepper

Cut lamb into 1-inch (2.5 cm) cubes and dredge in flour. In a large, heavy saucepan or Dutch oven, heat half of the bacon fat over high heat; add half of the lamb and cook until nicely browned. Transfer to a plate. Heat remaining bacon fat and brown remaining lamb in the same way. Return browned lamb to pan; add onion, carrots, celery, parsley, thyme, and bay leaf, and season with salt and pepper to taste. Add just enough water to cover meat and vegetables. Bring to a boil, cover, and reduce heat to medium-low. Simmer stew for 1½ hours or until meat is tender. Remove bay leaf before serving.

Six to eight servings

TIP: Stew may be refrigerated for up to 2 days.

A Picnic Marker

Huge boulders act as landmarks throughout the townships. A large rock on Miltimore Road near West Brome is engraved with a little piece of local history. The founders of the Brome County Historical Society rolled it out of the nearby woods in 1899 to mark the spot where Henry Collins, first settler to obtain a land grant in the county, put up the first log cabin in this area in 1795. Archives housed in Knowlton reveal that a celebratory picnic had been held on that spot two years earlier, on August 18, 1897, when the society was founded. Old-timers speculate that the picnic menu might have been pork sandwiches, doughnuts, butternut cake, Duchess apples, and—to wash it all down—apple cider, ginger beer, or raspberry vinegar. At haying time the cooling drink was oatmeal water, made by soaking rolled oats in water along with sugar, vinegar, ginger, and maple syrup. Imperial drink was another beverage—a combination of lemon juice and rind with sugar, epsom salts, and some tartaric and citric acid.

SALADE AUX PISSENLITS

Dandelion salad

On the first day of May, when dandelion leaves are young and tender, this salad is part of a traditional spring meal in the southeastern region of the Eastern Townships. A similar salad, sometimes including potatoes, can be found in the Champagne region of northern France. This recipe comes from a collection published by the Cercle de Fermières of Sainte-Edwidge. It is traditionally served with cheese and fresh bread.

> 8 cups (2 L) fresh young dandelion leaves,
>   stems trimmed
> 6 thin slices salt pork (about ¼ pound/125 g),
>   chopped
> 1 small onion, finely chopped
> 3 to 4 tablespoons (45 to 60 mL) white vinegar
> Salt and freshly ground pepper

Place dandelion leaves, torn in bite-size pieces, in a large salad bowl. In a heavy frying pan, fry salt pork over medium-high heat, stirring, for 5 minutes or until crisp. Remove from pan with slotted spoon and drain on paper towels. Add onion and vinegar to pan; bring to a boil. Remove from heat and let stand for 1 minute to cool slightly. Pour dressing over dandelion leaves and season with salt and pepper to taste. Add crisp, fried pork and toss. Serve at once.

Six servings

Winning Cheese

A landmark on Lake Memphramagog is the soaring tower of the Abbaye de Saint-Benoît-du-Lac. Here the Benedictine monks live a contemplative life within the abbey walls, work on their tranquil farm, and make excellent cheese, which they mark with a logo of a black-robed monk. Recently upgrading their cheese-making with new staff from the outside world, they perfected their new Bleu Bénédictin brand, winning a Canadian Grand Prix award from the Dairy Farmers of Canada for the best cheese made with cows' milk. The abbey shop, which can be reached at (819) 843-4080, sells the monks' cheeses and apple cider; both products are also available at the corner store in nearby Austin.

OMELETTE AUX CHAMPIGNONS SAUVAGES

Wild mushroom omelette

Jean-Yves Prod'homme, who runs the celebrated L'Aubergade restaurant in Granby, picks his own wild mushrooms in nearby forests. Long specializing in regional meats and vegetables, the French-born chef grows his own herbs by his door.

5 tablespoons (75 mL) butter
4 ounces (125 g) chopped fresh chanterelle
  mushrooms*
1 large shallot, chopped
5 eggs
1 to 2 tablespoons (15 to 30 mL) chopped
  fresh chives
Salt and freshly ground pepper

*Substitute 4 ounces (125 g) white mushrooms and 2 packages (14 g each) of dried porcini mushrooms, soaked in water, then drained and patted dry.

In a heavy 10-inch (25 cm) non-stick frying pan, heat 2 tablespoons (25 mL) of the butter over medium–high heat. Cook mushrooms and shallot, stirring, for 3 minutes or until mushrooms release their liquid. Transfer to a bowl and let cool slightly.

In a bowl, beat eggs. Stir in mushroom mixture and chives; season with salt and pepper. Add remaining butter to the pan and heat over high heat. When butter is sizzling, add egg mixture. Cook omelette, lifting edges with a metal spatula as egg mixture begins to set, and tipping liquid egg

A Giant Omelette

Call it a 10,000-egg omelette or a giant batch of scrambled eggs. By either name, the centrepiece of the annual June 24th egg bash in Granby's town park is designed to provide the Confrérie Mondial des Chevaliers de l'Omelette Géante with a good time. The Quebec event, held on the province's Fête Nationale holiday, is one of six such celebrations in towns as far away as Europe, Louisiana, and the south Pacific. Confrérie members, dressed up in chefs' whites, ribbons, and medals, use a forklift to set a vast metal frying pan over a bonfire, then use power drills to beat eggs by the bucketful. Their spatulas are wooden paddles big enough for canoeing (photo opposite). The hundreds watching the action are offered free servings. The cook-in recreates a big omelette

mixture towards the edge of the pan until mixture is almost all set in the centre. Fold one half of the omelette over the other and tip out of the pan onto a warm serving plate. Serve at once.

Two servings

Napoleon once served his army. The celebration is La Francophonie at its most amicable. For information, call (450) 372-7273 or (800) 567-7273.

LONGE DE VEAU RÔTIE ET FRICASSÉE DE CHAMPIGNONS SAUVAGES

Roast loin of veal with wild mushrooms

Alain Labrie of Auberge Hatley gathers wild mushrooms in the woods around North Hatley to enhance his regional specialties. He uses herbs from the village's hydroponic herb farm, Domaine de la Cressonière, in his cuisine. Serve with browned small round potatoes.

> 6 tablespoons (90 mL) extra-virgin olive oil
> 2 tablespoons (30 mL) fresh thyme
> 2 tablespoons (30 mL) fresh basil
> 1¼ pounds (600 g) boneless loin of veal
> 4 tablespoons (60 mL) butter
> 3 shallots, finely chopped
> ½ cup (125 mL) port wine
> 4 cups (1 L) duck or chicken stock
> 5 small new potatoes, boiled, quartered
> 1¼ pounds (600 g) wild mushrooms*
> 2 tablespoons (30 mL) finely chopped fresh tarragon

*Use chanterelles, cèpes, and morels. Or substitute oyster, shiitake, and button mushrooms, about 200 g of each.

In a food processor, purée 4 tablespoons (60 mL) oil, thyme, and basil. Place veal in a heavy plastic bag, add herb marinade, close bag tightly, and refrigerate for up to 1 day.

Using a heavy frying pan, heat 1 tablespoon (15 mL) of the butter over medium-low heat and cook shallots for about 5 minutes or until softened. Increase heat to medium-high and stir in port. Add duck stock and bring to a boil. Cook until mixture is reduced to about 1¼ cups (300 mL). Set aside.

Remove veal from marinade and pat dry with paper towels. In a heavy frying pan, heat remaining oil over high heat. Sear meat about 5 to 7 minutes per side until nicely browned. (If frying pan handle is not heatproof, cover handle with aluminum foil.) Place pan in oven preheated to 400°F (200°C) and roast meat for 10 minutes or until desired degree of doneness. Remove from oven and let stand for 5 minutes.

Meanwhile, in another large, heavy frying pan, heat 2 tablespoons (30 mL) butter over medium heat and brown potatoes on all sides; set aside and keep warm. If necessary, add remaining 1 tablespoon (15 mL) butter to pan and, when hot, add mushrooms and cook just until they release their liquid and begin to brown. Stir in pan juices from roasted veal and sprinkle with tarragon. Cook just until heated through.

Slice veal into thick slices and arrange on 4 warm serving plates. Spoon mushroom sauce over veal, accompany with potatoes, and serve at once.

Four servings

TIP: As indicated in recipe, meat is placed in marinade 24 hours in advance.

(819) 876-5115. Smaller but outstanding is L'Aubergine, a tiny inn at Knowlton's Landing north of Mansonville, which can be reached at (450) 292-3246, and the Sutton B and B called Auberge Le St. Amour, which runs a fine restaurant on the spacious main floor; (450) 538-6188.

ROULADE DE TRUITE "DES BOBINES"

Trout rolls, oriental style

The Eastern Townships have several fish farms, providing Chef Alain Labrie with trout for this recipe, which is often on the menu at Auberge Hatley.

> 4 trout fillets, skinned, about 5 ounces (150 g) each
> 10 tablespoons (150 mL) extra-virgin olive oil
> 1 tablespoon (15 mL) tamari or soy sauce
> 6 tablespoons (90 mL) chopped, fresh coriander
> 1 teaspoon (5 mL) finely chopped fresh gingerroot
> 1 stem lemongrass, white bottom portion only, minced*
> 10 ounces (300 g) green beans
> 1¼ cups (300 mL) dry white wine
> 4 large shallots, minced
> 1 tablespoon (15 mL) aged balsamic vinegar
> Sea salt and freshly ground pepper

*Substitute grated lemon rind or additional grated fresh ginger.

Arrange trout fillets in a shallow dish just large enough to hold the fillets in a single layer. In a bowl, combine 4 tablespoons (60 mL) of the oil, tamari, 2 tablespoons (30 mL) coriander, gingerroot, and lemongrass; spread over trout. Cover and let marinate for 2 hours in the refrigerator.

In a food processor or blender, purée 4 tablespoons (60 mL) of the oil and the remaining coriander, and reserve in a bowl. Blanch beans in a saucepan of boiling, salted water for 2 minutes or until crisp-tender. Drain and rinse under cold water to chill.

Remove fish fillets from marinade and pat dry with paper towels. Roll up into tight rolls, securing each roll with a toothpick. In a stainless steel saucepan just large enough to hold the trout rolls, add white wine and bring to a boil. Add trout rolls, reduce heat to medium, and poach the fish for 3 minutes or until just opaque; do not overcook. Transfer fish to a hot platter and keep warm.

In a large heavy frying pan, heat remaining 2 tablespoons (30 mL) oil and sauté beans and shallots, stirring, for 3 minutes or until beans are heated through and shallots are tender. Arrange trout rolls on 4 warm serving plates. Surround with beans. Drizzle with oil–coriander mixture and balsamic vinegar, and season with salt and pepper to taste. Serve at once.

Four servings

TIP: Beans may be blanched up to 2 hours in advance.

French bread specialist Benoit Fradette, who leaves his flourishing Montreal bakery Le Fromentier on weekends to bake for a lavishly stocked delicatessen called Le Rumeur Affamée. One of the sweet treats at this shop is from Sucreries de l'Érable in Frelighsburg, maker of a celebrated maple syrup pie. Or you can shop in the Frelighsburg restaurant-gift shop designed to look like an old-time general store. Abercorn Boulangerie Croissanterie makes an excellent assortment of oatmeal breads, muffins, and butter tarts. And Lennoxville's Greens bakery, half a century old, makes a best-selling shredded wheat loaf.

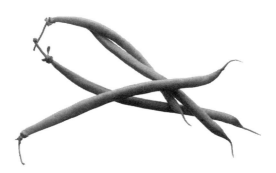

BISCUITS AU SIROP D'ÉRABLE

Maple cookies

Museums with Flavour

Maple syrup in the spring, apples in the fall—these annual harvests have inspired the Missisquoi Historical Society in Stanbridge East to celebrate twice a year with a spring maple brunch and an autumn apple pie festival. Fundraisers for the Missisquoi Museum, housed in a mill built in 1830 over the Missisquoi River, these two events are sweet traditions throughout the district. More than 1,000 line up on a fall Sunday afternoon for apple pie with ice cream, cheese, and a chaser of apple cider or juice (for information, call [450] 248-3153). Further south in Stanstead is Carrollcroft, a handsome 1859 granite mansion. It's now the Curtis-Colby Museum, complete with its original 19th century furnishings and serving afternoon tea in summer. At Lennoxville is Uplands, a gracious red brick house dating from 1862, now operated as the Uplands Cultural and Heritage Centre. Summer teas are served to recreate a custom of 19th century family life.

When Pauline Jacques, who runs the Granby cooking school Les Ateliers de Pauline, was growing up, she remembers both her mother and grandmother making these cookies to serve with maple mousse. The family recipe is based on one from her treasured cookbook, *Cuisinière de la Reverende Mère Caron,* first published in 1878 by the Sisters of Providence.

1 cup (250 mL) butter or shortening, at room temperature
1 cup (250 mL) brown sugar
2 eggs, beaten
⅓ cup (75 mL) maple syrup
1 teaspoon (5 mL) vanilla extract
3½ cups (875 mL) cake and pastry flour (approximate)
2 teaspoons (10 mL) baking powder
½ teaspoon (2 mL) salt

In a large bowl, cream butter with brown sugar until fluffy. Beat in eggs, maple syrup, and vanilla until well combined.

In another bowl, combine 3 cups (750 mL) of the flour with baking powder and salt. Stir dry ingredients into creamed mixture, along with enough of the remaining ½ cup (125 mL) flour, until dough leaves the sides of the bowl and forms a ball. Cover dough and chill until firm, about 2 hours.

On a lightly floured surface, thinly roll out dough and cut into desired shapes using cookie cutters.

Place on lightly greased baking sheets and bake in a preheated 350°F (180°C) oven for 8 to 10 minutes or until edges are lightly browned and crisp.

Makes 5 to 6 dozen cookies

MOUSSE À L'ÉRABLE

Sometimes called a mousse, this sauce is more like a "meringue italienne," says Pauline Jacques, who considers it a perfect topping for Maple Cookies (see page 94). She makes the latter in the shape of maple leaves.

> 1 cup (250 mL) maple syrup
> 1 egg white
> Pinch cream of tartar

Make sauce no more than an hour before serving.

In a small saucepan, bring maple syrup to a boil over medium-high heat. Let boil until syrup reaches the firm ball stage, 248°F (120°C) on a candy thermometer.

In a bowl, using an electric mixer, beat egg white with cream of tartar until stiff peaks form. Pour the boiling syrup into the beaten egg white in a thin steady stream, continuing to beat at high speed for 3 to 4 minutes or until sauce is smooth and shiny. Spoon into individual serving dishes and serve accompanied with Maple Cookies.

Makes about 1 cup (250 mL) sauce

Harvests to Celebrate

The season of harvest fairs has its stars, both new–the Gaelic bagpipe and Scotch-tasting event launched recently in mid-August called the Scottish Festival of Gould ([819] 877-5688)–and old-Big Brome Fair ([450] 242-3976), held every Labour Day weekend since 1856. By mid-August, the apple orchards start opening for you-pick customers in three principle areas (around Hemmingford, Dunham, and Saint-Hilaire), followed in mid-September by Quebec's 23 wineries. Tourist offices distribute a detailed map to the wine region, called La Route des Vins (www.vignerons-du-quebec.com). During fall, wineries offer tastings, sell their wines, and run restaurants so you can try vintages with food before you buy more to take home.

GÂTEAU REINE ÉLISABETH

Queen Elizabeth cake

Dates and nuts are always part of this Townships cake. The icing usually contains brown sugar and more nuts. Coconut is an option. Legend has it Queen Elizabeth, the Queen Mother, shared the recipe with members of the Women's Institutes to use as a fundraiser for charitable purposes. Her Majesty's lady-in-waiting has denied this story. Linda Bresee of Sutton Junction has won prizes for this recipe at Big Brome Fair, where the cake has its own category.

Bridges and Barns

Covered bridges abound and so do round barns, the former well marked on road signs, the latter requiring a search. Look for the bridges at Adamsville, Compton, Cowansville, Eaton, Milby, and Saint-Isidore d'Auckland. The most unusual round barn is a 12-sided structure in Mystic. West Brome, Mansonville, Barnston, and Ways Mills are some other locations for these barns, most still in use. The original idea was that the design was safer because the devil wouldn't be able to hide in such a barn. Economy was the real reason, say farmers. The cattle have stalls around the

1 cup (250 mL) water
1 cup (250 mL) chopped dates
1 teaspoon (5 mL) baking soda
¼ cup (60 mL) butter
1 cup (250 mL) granulated sugar
1 egg
1 teaspoon (5 mL) vanilla extract
1½ cups (375 mL) all–purpose flour
1 teaspoon (5 mL) baking powder
¼ teaspoon (1 mL) salt
½ cup (125 mL) chopped walnuts
Broiled Icing (recipe follows)

Place water in a saucepan and bring to a boil. Remove from heat and add dates and baking soda. Let stand until lukewarm. In a bowl, cream butter with sugar until fluffy; beat in egg and vanilla until smooth. Stir in date mixture. In another bowl, combine flour, baking powder, and salt. Stir dry ingredients into creamed mixture until combined. Fold in walnuts. Pour batter into a greased 9-inch (23 cm) square baking pan. Bake in a preheated 350°F (180°C) oven for 40 to 45 minutes or until a tester inserted in centre comes out clean.

While cake is still warm, spread with Broiled Icing and place under a preheated broiler for 2 to 3 minutes or until lightly browned.

Makes one 9-inch (23 cm) square cake

Broiled Icing
⅓ cup (75 mL) brown sugar
3 tablespoons (45 mL) butter
2 tablespoons (30 mL) whipping cream
½ cup (125 mL) sweetened, flaked coconut
½ cup (125 mL) chopped walnuts (optional)

In a small saucepan, combine brown sugar, butter, cream, coconut, and nuts, if desired. Bring to a boil over medium heat; boil for 3 minutes. Makes about 1¼ cups (300 mL).

circle, heads toward the centre where their hay is dropped conveniently from the loft above. Among architectural curios is a pig barn on a hillside above Lake Massawippi, which has been turned into a summer theatre called "The Piggery" (www.piggery.com).

MOUSSE AUX FRAISES

Strawberry mousse

When strawberries are at their ripest and best, pastry chef Angèle Racicot of Hovey Manor in North Hatley blends the fruit into this simple mousse. If the fruit needs a lift, her addition of orange juice does the trick. Serve the mousse in individual glasses or line a springform pan with ladyfingers and fill the centre with this succulent mixture. The surplus egg whites can be used to make meringues to go with more sliced, sugared strawberries.

2 cups (500 mL) fresh, sliced strawberries
  (1 heaping pint)
¾ cup (175 mL) granulated sugar
2 egg yolks
1 package (7 g) unflavoured gelatin
1 cup (250 mL) milk
½ cup (125 mL) fresh orange juice
1 teaspoon (5 mL) vanilla extract
1 cup (250 mL) whipping cream
⅓ cup (75 mL) strawberry, raspberry, or
  red–currant jelly (optional)

Set aside 1 cup (250 mL) sliced strawberries for topping. Place remaining 1 cup (250 mL) berries in food processor or blender with 3 tablespoons (45 mL) of the sugar and purée until smooth; set aside. In a bowl, using an electric mixer, beat remaining sugar with egg yolks for 3 minutes or until very light and creamy.

Place milk in a medium saucepan and sprinkle with gelatin; let stand for 2 minutes to soften. Place over medium-low heat, stirring, until milk is hot and bubbles form around edge; do not permit to boil. Pour hot milk mixture into sugar and egg mixture, whisking constantly. Return mixture to saucepan and cook about 2 minutes, continuing to whisk, until custard thickens slightly; do not let mixture boil. Stir in orange juice and vanilla. Transfer to a large bowl and stir in the puréed strawberries. Refrigerate, stirring occasionally, until mixture cools and is the consistency of raw egg white; be careful not to let mixture set. In a bowl, whip cream until stiff peaks form and fold into custard. Pour into individual serving dishes. Refrigerate for 3 hours or until set. Just before serving, heat jelly in a small saucepan until melted. Stir in remaining sliced berries. Top each serving with berries and a dollop of the whipped cream, if desired.

Six servings

TIP: Mousse may be made up to 8 hours in advance.

SAGUENAY-LAC SAINT-JEAN

There's an inn on the Saguenay River where the tablemats list 21 names, many of them Tremblays, others Villeneuve, Simard, Harvey, Blackburn, and Boudreau. These men were the first white settlers in this northern wilderness. It had come to be called the kingdom of the Saguenay, a description given to Jacques Cartier by his Indian guides when he explored the mouth of the river in 1535. "The 21," as the pioneers are called, paddled north in 1838 from Charlevoix to settle on the site of the town of La Baie and start the region's logging industry. The modern inn is called Auberge des 21, and chef-owner Marcel Bouchard is a proud descendant of one of those settlers. Their history is depicted each summer when La Baie hosts an historical pageant called La Fabuleuse Histoire d'un Royaume (the fabulous history of a kingdom). Nearby on the Saguenay is one of the sites of *Black Robe,* the 1991 movie based on Brian Moore's book about the Jesuits and natives in 17th century New France. Called the Site de tournage "Robe Noire," it's staffed by guides who explain the region's history going back 5,000 years.

Driving north across the Laurentides park, I passed mountains and lakes as uninhabited as the wilderness depicted in *Black Robe.* Marcel Bouchard's menus include foods both natives and French might have eaten in the 17th century. Dining on his windowed terrace on a summer evening, I started with smoked salmon, a touch of maple syrup in the cream sauce. Rare-cooked caribou chops were trimmed with wild pleurotte mushrooms and tiny flowers carved from raw turnip. Dessert was a wild strawberry mousse with a rhubarb compote and a tracing of chocolate.

Marcel likes to serve wild mushrooms that he and friends pick in undisclosed locations. "We keep all the places very secret. A mycologist can share his wife, but not his mushroom places," the chef said with a grin. Each October, he cooks a seven-course dinner for about 150 members of the Club des Mycologues du Saguenay. "Even dessert contains mushrooms," he said, describing how he makes the nut-flavoured petit marasme mushroom into a mousse or tart.

The cuisine of this region includes some of the most distinctive dishes in the province, for the population was isolated and their original home cooking altered only by the local ingredients they found. Until the last half-century, contact with the outside world came only through the English-speaking bosses of the big paper and power companies. The kingdom even has its own fish, the prized, land-locked salmon called the ouananiche, once plentiful in Lac Saint-Jean, but now so scarce that it's farm-raised at Saint-Félicien.

Chef Diane Tremblay serves it at her little restaurant, Le Privilège, south of Chicoutimi. One summer evening, she prepared me the fish in a ceviche with morsels of green and red bell peppers, smoked salmon, and strawberries. Her source for local fruit and vegetables is right across the road from her 1861 clapboard at the Gobeil family market garden. Yvon Gobeil, showing off his yellow zucchini and purple basil, said he likes to give a sunflower to each of his Sunday shoppers. This man, fifth generation to farm his terrain, is passionate about his work, and about his pine forest with its rows of trees that resemble, as he sees it, the aisle of a cathedral. It's the same kind of pride demonstrated by the Perron family, cheese makers at Saint-Prime since 1895. For much of the past century, they exported almost all their Cheddar cheese to England. Nowadays, with their aged Cheddar winning prizes, more than half of it sells in Canada and they have opened a little museum to explain the Cheddar-making traditions of earlier times.

French-born Chef Daniel Pachon of Jonquière uses Perron cheese and a big variety of other local foods. Chef-owner of Villa Pachon, he cooked me a dinner that began with a thick slab of his own smoked salmon, served hot with a maple vinegar sauce, fresh dill from his herb garden, and orange marmalade. Tender chops of "cerf rouge" (red deer) had a red currant sauce touched with balsamic vinegar. Dessert combined the region's favourite berries—blueberries, raspberries, and a chocolate-coated strawberry set in a crisp-baked cookie basket.

Blueberries are the best-known food in this area, so much so that residents are nick-named "les bleuets." If you drive around Lac Saint-Jean in August, you see a grey-blue haze to many a field as the tiny, wild berries turn plump and sweet. They aren't really wild; growers explain they encourage the wild plants by setting fire to the blueberry fields each spring. That custom began after a huge fire ravaged the countryside in 1870, with the unexpected result of a big blueberry crop the next year. (Blueberries are some-times called "fils du feu," son of the fire, and something out-of-date is described as "before the fire.") Fertilizers and bees help the "bleuetières" and—unless frost strikes at blossom time—a lavish crop ripens in time for the annual August blueberry festival at Mistassini. Then, blueberry warehouses bustle with pickers arriving with crates of the tiny fruit for either transport to market or freezing. Les Gâteries du Lac, a shop north-west of Mistassini, starts selling the annual chocolate-coated blueberry candy and blue-berry jam made by the local Trappist monks. The arrival of the candy is eagerly await-ed in specialty food stores all over the province each August. But not all blueberry cui-sine is sweet. Chef Marcel Bouchard makes a blueberry and cucumber relish to serve with terrines and cold meat. He acquired the recipe from a Montagnais Indian woman.

Aumonières de homard aux pistaches et poivres verts (Lobster in pastry pouches with red pistachio sauce) by Chef François Létourneau.

© François Létourneau/*The Gazette*

Mist and mountains line the Laurentians' Jacques-Cartier River.

© Heiko Wittenborn/Tourisme Québec heikow@sympatico.ca

Salade d'oie au celerirave
(Goose salad) by Chef Alain Pignard.

The quaint resort of Tremblant in ski season.

Selle d'agneau rôtie au
giroffe (Lamb roast) by
Chef Normand Laprise.

The brilliant colours of autumn
surround an old ice house in
the Eastern Townships.

Foie gras de canard sauce hydromel (Duck foie gras with honey wine sauce) by Chef Anne Desjardins.

© Tedd Church/*The Gazette*

An Inukshuk guides travellers outside Kuujjuaq, northern Quebec.

© Heiko Wittenborn/Tourisme Québec heikow@sympatico.ca

Tarte au sucre (Sugar pie)
from the Eastern Townships.

© Gordon Beck

A busy street in Quartier
Petit-Champlain in Quebec
City's lower town.

© Elizabeth Lambert

Chèvre frais et tomates confites salade folle de roquette (Tomato goat cheese appetizer) by Chef Alain Labrie.

© Gordon Beck

Colourful canoes at rest in Parc Mont Tremblant.

© Heiko Wittenborn/Tourisme Québec heikow@sympatico.ca

Soupe au melon (Melon soup) by Chef Anne Desjardins.

© Guillaume Pouliot/ L'Eau à la Bouche

A herd of caribou. © Louis Gagnon/Tourisme Québec

Lettuces and pansies from an organic farm at Athelstan, southwest of Montreal.

© Gordon Beck/*The Gazette*

The *pigeonnier* reflected at les Quatre Vents gardens in La Malbaie, Québec.

© Elizabeth Lambert

SOUPE À L'IVROGNE

Drunkard's soup

Economical, easy to make, and satisfying, this soup is thus named because it could sustain a drunkard's family when food money was short. Other theories are that it's a fast meal to make when you have a hangover or that it's a cure for a hangover. Micheline Mongrain-Dontigny included it in *100 recettes pour le Saguenay-Lac-St-Jean à cuisiner,* the cookbook she wrote to mark the 150th anniversary of the 1838 settlement of the Saguenay-Lac Saint-Jean region.

TIP: Soup may be prepared several hours in advance, up to the point mixture is transferred to saucepan. An hour before serving, add beef stock and herbs and complete recipe.

2 tablespoons (30 mL) salted herbs, commercially
   prepared or homemade (see p. 167)
¼ pound (125 g) salt pork, diced
3 large onions, chopped
6 slices white bread, cubed
8 cups (2 L) beef stock
Salt and freshly ground pepper

Rinse herbs in cold water, then drain. In a large, cast-iron frying pan over medium heat, cook salt pork, stirring, for 5 minutes or until crisp and brown. Add onions and cook, stirring, for 6 to 8 minutes or until golden. Add bread cubes to the frying pan; toss to coat well. Place frying pan in a preheated 350°F (180°C) oven for 15 minutes to toast bread lightly.

Transfer mixture to a large, heavy saucepan. Add beef stock and salted herbs. Bring to a boil, reduce heat, and simmer, covered, for 1 hour. Adjust seasoning with salt and pepper to taste.

Eight to ten servings

SOUPE AUX GOURGANES

Bean soup

TIP: Soup may be completed, refrigerated, solid fat removed, and reheated.

The big, red-streaked bean called the "gourgane" was brought by the earliest settlers from France, from the Marais region near Paris, and became a staple, first in the Charlevoix region and then in the Saguenay. Each year Lac Saint-Jean growers dry and export millions of dollars worth of these beans to countries around the world. This recipe belongs to Jeannine Renouf, a talented Jonquière cook.

> 2 pounds (1 kg) fresh or frozen gourgane or
>   fava beans
> 1 onion, finely chopped
> 1 carrot, finely chopped
> ¼ cup (60 mL) uncooked barley, rinsed
> ¼ pound (125 g) salt pork, in 1 piece
> Salt and freshly ground pepper
> ½ teaspoon (2 mL) dried savory
> 2 tablespoons (30 mL) chopped fresh parsley
> 2 tablespoons (30 mL) chopped fresh chives

If using fresh beans, shell and discard pods. (Some cooks believe that removing the tiny seed at the end of each bean prevents the soup from turning grey as it cooks.) In a large, heavy saucepan, combine beans, onion, carrot, barley, and salt pork.

Add enough water to cover ingredients by 2 inches (5 cm). Add savory and bring to a boil; reduce heat and simmer, covered, for 1½ to 2 hours or until beans are tender. Add parsley and chives; season with salt and pepper to taste. Cook for 15 minutes more. (Remove salt pork, cut into small pieces and return to soup, if desired.) Serve hot.

Eight servings

CÔTES DE VEAU DE CHARLEVOIX ET MIGNERON

Charlevoix veal with cheese

Mushrooms and the Baie-Saint-Paul cheese, Le Migneron, are used by Chef Marcel Bouchard of Auberge des 21 to accent veal.

3 tablespoons (45 mL) butter
2 veal chops, each 8 to 10 ounces (250 to 300 g)
2 thin slices Migneron or Oka cheese
4 ounces (125 g) portobello mushrooms, sliced
4 ounces (125 g) oyster mushrooms, ends trimmed
2 shallots, finely chopped
3 tablespoons (45 mL) honey wine (mead) or
    white wine
¼ cup (60 mL) whipping cream
Juice of ½ lemon

In a large, heavy frying pan, heat 1 tablespoon (15 mL) butter over high heat and brown veal chops on both sides. Transfer pan to lower rack of preheated 375°F (190°C) oven for 3 minutes for medium–rare. Add a slice of cheese to each chop and return to oven for 2 minutes more or until cheese melts. Transfer meat to a hot platter and keep warm.

In same pan, heat 1 tablespoon (15 mL) of the butter over medium–high heat and cook portobello mushrooms, stirring, for 2 minutes. Add oyster mushrooms and cook, stirring, for 2 minutes. Transfer mushrooms to a bowl and keep warm. Reduce heat to medium and add remaining butter to frying pan; add shallots and cook, stirring, for 2 minutes or until softened. Add honey wine and simmer until reduced to a glaze. Add cream and lemon juice; cook over medium–high heat, stirring, until sauce has slightly reduced, adding any veal juices. Serve veal chops on warmed plates, topped with sauce and mushrooms.

Two servings

Where to Stay

Auberge des 21, a big, comfortable, modern inn at La Baie has become popular with both local people and business visitors, to the point where chef-owner Marcel Bouchard must constantly change his menu to satisfy guests who dine there more than once a week. Cuisine is excellent. Ask for a room "on the fiord" so you can watch weather changes on the Saguenay River. 621 Mars St., La Baie; (418) 697-2121; (800) 363-7298; moderately expensive. Villa Pachon, a handsome 1911 Tudor-style residence on the outskirts of Jonquière, was once the Price paper company's guest house. It's now a small inn run by French chef Daniel Pachon and his wife, Carole Tremblay. Cuisine is excellent. Dinner is served in the one-time drawing room, and breakfast in the rustic, log-walled lounge. 1904 Perron St., Jonquière; (418) 542-3568; (888) 922-3568; moderately expensive.

TOURTIÈRE DU SAGUENAY

Saguenay meat pie

Tourtière du Saguenay

Unlike other tourtières, which are shallow tarts of ground meat and onions, this dish is composed of layers of cubed meat and potato in a pastry crust. It's often compared to the layered casserole called "cipaille" or "cipâte" in other regions. In the Saguenay, that name usually refers to a layered blueberry tart. One theory is that the local tourtière was derived from the "pâté de famille" found in older, settled regions along the St. Lawrence River. This family meat pie is also made of cubed or thinly sliced meat and layered with sliced or minced onions and carrots. The closest relative to the usual tourtière in Saguenay-Lac Saint-Jean is "pâté à la viande," a shallow pie made with ground meat, potatoes, and spices.

The most distinctive dish of the region is this combination of cubed meats, onions, and potatoes, baked in layers in a deep, pastry-lined casserole. Marcelle Sénéchal of Jonquière assembles her pie in easy stages, then bakes it for 3 to 4 hours or, if it suits her, at a low temperature all day long. She and her husband, Gérard, consider this dish special-occasion fare for family and friends.

> 1 pound (500 g) pork
> 3 pounds (1.5 kg) assorted meats*
> 1 large onion, chopped
> Salt and freshly ground pepper
> 6 pounds (3 kg) potatoes, peeled and cubed
>   (9 to 10 cups/2.5 L)
> Ground cinnamon
> Pastry for 2 double-crust, 9-inch (23 cm) pies
>   (recipe p. 15)

*One-third beef, one-third veal, and one-third chicken, partridge, or hare are suggested.

Cut meat into 1-inch (2.5 cm) cubes and place in a large bowl with onion. Season with salt and pepper to taste; cover and refrigerate overnight. Place potatoes in another large bowl; add water to cover and refrigerate overnight. Cut pastry into 2 pieces, one slightly larger than the other. On a lightly floured board, roll out the larger ball of dough so it is slightly less than ¼ inch (5 mm) thick. Using a deep, heavy casserole dish, either a 14-inch (35 cm) oval or a 12-inch (30 cm) round shape, line the bottom and sides with pastry. Drain potatoes. Arrange alternate layers of meat and potatoes in the pastry-lined casserole, sprinkling each layer lightly with salt, pepper, and a little cinnamon. Add just enough cold water to cover the mixture. Roll out smaller piece of pastry just large enough to cover the top of the casserole; trim and pinch edges to seal. (Decorate with an extra border of pastry, if desired.) Cut steam vents in pastry top.

Bake in a preheated 425°F (220°C) oven for 1 hour. When pastry turns golden, cover with casserole lid or double layer of aluminum foil, reduce temperature to 300°F (150°C), and cook slowly for 2 to 3 hours more.

Ten to twelve servings

TIP: As indicated in the recipe, pastry and meat are prepared the day before and refrigerated.

GRILLADE D'AGNEAU SUR SA COROLLE DE LÉGUMES

Lamb with baked vegetables

Chef Diane Tremblay (photo opposite) practises an elaborate type of local cuisine at her restaurant, Le Privilège, near Chicoutimi. Her colourful vegetable and cheese creation accents local lamb chops.

> 3 ripe plum tomatoes, thinly sliced
> 1 medium zucchini, thinly sliced
> 1 leek, white part only, sliced
> 4 ounces (125 g) aged Cheddar cheese*, sliced
> 6 tablespoons (90 mL) olive oil
> ½ cup (125 mL) finely chopped fresh basil leaves
> Salt and freshly ground pepper
> 1 shallot, minced
> 1 clove garlic, crushed
> 8 lamb chops

*Aged Perron Cheddar from Saint-Prime is recommended.

Place a sheet of parchment paper or aluminum foil on a baking sheet. Using a round 9-inch (23 cm) cake pan as a guide, trace a circle on the paper or foil. Arrange alternating slices of tomatoes and zucchini, 1 or 2 slices of leek, and 1 slice of cheese just inside the edge of the circle. Continue alternating vegetables and cheese in the same way until the circle is filled. Season with salt and pepper and drizzle with 1 tablespoon (15 mL) of the oil. Place baking sheet in centre of preheated 350°F (180°C) oven for 35 to 40 minutes. In a bowl, mix the basil with 3 tablespoons (45 mL) oil and spread on the vegetables, then return to oven for 2 minutes or until basil wilts.

Five minutes before the end of baking time, heat
2 tablespoons (30 mL) oil in a large, heavy frying pan
over medium-high heat. Add shallot and garlic and cook
for 1 minute, then add lamb chops and sear for 2 minutes
a side. Remove lamb to a warm platter. Season with salt
and pepper.

To serve, cut the circle of vegetables into 4 portions
and place each on a heated serving plate. Add 2 lamb
chops to each plate and serve.

Four servings

TIP: The circle of vegetables and cheese may be assembled,
but not baked, up to 4 hours in advance.

OUANANICHE FARCIE AU FOUR

Baked stuffed ouananiche

The celebrated ouananiche, fresh-water ancestor of the salmon, once made Lac Saint-Jean a fisherman's paradise. But the dams and water pollution of the rivers that flow into the great northern lake have caused this fish to become more legend than habit. Older cooks remember feasting on ouananiche, stuffed with slices of lemon and hard-boiled eggs, then baked with a generous coating of butter. Another popular stuffing is made with bread crumbs, mushrooms, and white wine.

1 whole ouananiche, salmon, or trout
   (3 pounds/1.5 kg)
Salt and freshly ground white pepper
2 tablespoons (30 mL) butter
¼ cup (60 mL) finely chopped onion
¼ cup (60 mL) finely chopped celery
1 small garlic clove, minced
1 cup (250 mL) sliced mushrooms
2 tablespoons (30 mL) chopped fresh parsley
1 cup (250 mL) soft, fresh bread crumbs
Melted butter or oil
½ cup (125 mL) white wine

Clean fish; rinse under cold running water. Remove head and tail. Pat dry with paper towels. Season cavity with salt and pepper.

In a large frying pan, melt butter over medium heat and cook onion, celery, and garlic, stirring, for 5 minutes or until softened. Add mushrooms and parsley; cook, stirring, for 1 minute. Stir in bread crumbs; season with salt and pepper. Stuff fish with bread mixture, close the opening with skewers, and lace up with string. Brush fish lightly with melted butter or oil. Arrange in a large buttered or oiled baking pan. Pour wine over fish and bake in a pre-heated 400°F (200°C) oven for 25 to 35 minutes, basting often, until fish flakes when tested with a fork.

Six to eight servings

TIP: Fish and stuffing may be prepared and refrigerated. Stuff fish just before baking.

PÂTE À LA VIANDE

Ground meat pie

Convent Memories

Quebec's first domestic science school was opened by the Ursuline nuns in 1882 at their convent in Roberval on Lac Saint-Jean. Called L'Ecole Menagère de Roberval, it became famous throughout Quebec. Memories of convent life were vivid for the late Constance Garneau of Montreal, who, with three of her sisters, was a student at the school from 1912 to 1914. "We entered a medieval world," she recalled. "Except for electric light and running water, life here was lived as it had been when the Ursuline Order was founded in the 16th century."

Besides reading, writing, and arithmetic, the students, mostly daughters of farmers, were taught how to raise cows, pigs, sheep, hens, and even bees, how to grow their own vegetables and fruits, how to weave and spin wool, and how to cook and preserve food.

The girls were taught how to prepare for the long winters, when temperatures went down as low as

There's a vigorous debate among cooks in Saguenay over the meats, vegetables, and seasonings in this pie, a cousin of the tourtière of other parts of Quebec. Monique Girard-Solomita, a Montreal journalist from Roberval, calls it "heresy" to add potatoes. Some versions include beef, salt pork, cloves, or dry mustard. Monique recommends serving her recipe with gherkins and pickled beets.

¾ pound (375 g) ground pork
¾ pound (375 g) ground veal
1 tablespoon (15 mL) butter
1 medium onion, chopped
2 cups (500 mL) veal or beef stock
¼ teaspoon (1 mL) cinnamon
1 bay leaf
1 teaspoon (5 mL) coarse salt
Freshly ground pepper
Pastry for double-crust, 9-inch (23 cm) pie (recipe p.15)

In a large, heavy saucepan over high heat, cook pork and veal, stirring to break up meat lumps, for 7 minutes or until no longer pink. Place meat in a strainer to drain fat; set meat aside. Add butter to saucepan over medium heat and cook onion, stirring, for 3 minutes or until softened. Return meat to pan and add stock, cinnamon, bay leaf, salt, and pepper to taste. Bring to a boil, reduce heat, and simmer, covered, for 2 to 2½ hours. Let cool.

On a lightly floured board, roll out half the dough thinly and line a 9-inch (23 cm) pie plate. Fill with meat mixture. Roll out remaining dough and place over filling; trim, crimp edges to seal, and cut steam vents in top. Bake in a preheated 400°F (200°C) oven for 15 minutes, then lower oven temperature to 350°F (180°C) and bake another 25 to 30 minutes or until top is lightly browned.

Eight servings

TIP: Pie may be completely prepared up to the point it is baked, then frozen for up to one month. Thaw in refrigerator before baking.

forty below zero. "A pig was slaughtered and we were shown how to make sausage and blood pudding. As soon as the real freeze-up came, quarters of beef, pork, chickens, and dozens of partridges and other game were put in cold places to freeze until needed."

To make the sausages, Mme Garneau remembered scalding and scrubbing "yards and yards" of pig's intestines with soap and water, seasoning great vats of blood with spices, then pouring the blood into the animal's gut. Learning how to roll pie dough, fry doughnuts, and bake cakes were more pleasant lessons.

The convent's bees would be brought indoors to spend the winter in the basement under her dormitory. "We were often told to walk softly so as not to disturb the bees. We could hear them buzzing under the floor," said Mme Garneau.

POUDING DU CHÔMEUR DE SAGUENAY

Brown sugar cake

An Abandoned Village

Only ghosts inhabit the clapboard houses that were once homes for workers at the company town Village Historique de Val-Jalbert. But the thundering waterfall that assaults your ears as you approach this long-gone settlement east of Roberval demonstrates the power that caused Damase Jalbert to build a mill on the Ouiatchouan River in 1901 and import workers to make pulp. At its peak, the company town had about 950 inhabitants. New owners closed the mill in 1927 and the buildings were left to crumble for almost half a century. Take stairs or a cable car to the top of the 72-metre waterfall, 21 metres higher than Niagara Falls. Visit the mill, convent school, and general store, where you can buy local crafts and refreshments. Open from early May to mid-October. Admission. For information call (418) 275-3132 or (888) 675-3132.

This super-sweet baked dessert takes its name from chômeur—"unemployed person." Gilles Lemieux of Arvida was unemployed when he submitted wife Diane's recipe for inclusion in a little cookbook published in 1986. Versions of the dessert turn up all over Quebec. In Saguenay-Lac Saint-Jean, the syrup is poured over the cake batter, rather than the reverse.

Base

1 cup (250 mL) all-purpose flour
1½ teaspoons (7 mL) baking powder
¼ teaspoon (1 mL) salt
⅓ cup (75 mL) butter or shortening, softened
⅔ cup (150 mL) granulated sugar
1 egg
1 teaspoon (5 mL) vanilla extract
⅓ cup (75 mL) milk

In a bowl, combine flour, baking powder, and salt. In another bowl, cream butter with granulated sugar until fluffy. Beat in egg and vanilla. Add dry ingredients alternately with milk to creamed mixture until combined. Spread batter evenly in a buttered 9-inch (23 cm) square baking pan.

Topping

1½ cups (375 mL) brown sugar
3 tablespoons (45 mL) all–purpose flour
2 tablespoons (30 mL) butter
2 cups (500 mL) water

In a saucepan, combine brown sugar, flour, butter, and water. Place over medium heat and bring to a boil, stirring, until slightly thickened. Pour over batter in baking pan. Do not mix.

Bake in a preheated 350°F (180°C) oven for 50 to 60 minutes or until top is golden and a tester inserted in the centre comes out clean.

Eight servings

A Unique Garden

You could be in one of Europe's palace gardens, until you notice many of the orderly beds of plants at Les Grands Jardins de Normandin (photo left) contain hundreds of leeks, ornamental cabbages, purple basil, and lettuce. Vegetables and herbs make up a big part of this 137-acre ornamental garden west of Lac Saint-Jean. Some plants flourish next to others because such pairings protect each from insects. There's an herb garden inspired by medieval designs, an English garden, moss and shrub gardens, an oriental mosaic bed modelled on designs from Mesopotamia in 3000 B.C., and a Parterre du Midi based on the gardens of 17th and 18th century Versailles. Open from June 24 to Labour Day. Admission. 1515 du Rocher Ave., Normandin; Call (418) 274-1993 or (800) 920-1993, or visit www.cigp.com/jardin.html.

POUDING RENVERSÉ DES BLEUETS

Blueberry upside-down pudding

Lemon-flavoured cake batter baked over fresh blueberries makes a perfect dessert. When I was immersed in French-language studies at Jonquière's Centre linguistique, Jeannine Renouf treated me to this recipe and also to a version she makes with wild raspberries. It was a delectable kind of immersion.

> 2 cups (500 mL) fresh or frozen unsweetened
>   blueberries
> ¾ cup (175 mL) granulated sugar
> 1 teaspoon (5 mL) grated lemon rind
> ¼ cup (60 mL) shortening
> 1 egg
> 1 teaspoon (5 mL) vanilla extract
> 1¼ cups (300 mL) all-purpose flour
> 1½ teaspoons (7 mL) baking powder
> ¼ teaspoon (1 mL) salt
> ⅔ cup (150 mL) milk
> Whipped or ice cream (optional)

In a buttered 8-inch (20 cm) square baking pan, combine blueberries, ¼ cup (50 mL) of the sugar, and lemon rind. In a bowl, cream shortening with remaining ½ cup (125 mL) sugar until fluffy. Beat in egg and vanilla. In another bowl, combine flour, baking powder, and salt. Stir in creamed mixture alternately with milk to make a smooth batter. Spoon over blueberries in pan and bake in a preheated 350°F (180°C) oven for about 40 minutes, or until a tester inserted in centre comes out clean. Let cool slightly; turn out onto serving plate. Cut in squares and serve warm or at room temperature, with whipped or ice cream, if desired.

Six to eight servings

CROUSTADE AUX BLEUETS

Blueberry oat crumble

This easy baked dessert comes from the recipe collection of Mme Guy Dupont of Arvida and was published in the Saguenay-Lac Saint-Jean cookbook *Le pinereau* by the late Cécile Roland Bouchard of Chicoutimi. It could be used with any fresh fruit in season.

4 cups (1 L) fresh or frozen blueberries
¾ cup (175 mL) granulated sugar
⅓ cup (75 mL) butter, softened
⅓ cup (75 mL) brown sugar
⅓ cup (75 mL) all–purpose flour
¾ cup (175 mL) rolled oats
Light cream

Spread blueberries evenly in a buttered 8- or 9-inch (20 or 23 cm) square baking pan. Sprinkle with granulated sugar. In a bowl, cream butter with brown sugar; stir in flour and rolled oats. Spread mixture evenly over fruit. Bake in a preheated 350°F (180°C) oven for 30 to 35 minutes or until top is golden brown. Serve warm with cream.

Six to eight servings

Blueberry Brix

Lac-Saint-Jean blueberries are tiny, less than a quarter-inch (5 mm) in diameter, with a delicate sweet-sour taste. A low-bush variety, they pack a far bigger flavour punch than many of the plumper, cultivated varieties, because, explains McGill University plant scientist Deborah Buszard, of the brix. That's the scientific term for the amount of natural sugar in the fruit. Wild blueberries were bred in a larger size for a more economical yield, so the original flavour is therefore diluted. In the Saguenay region, blue pearls, as they're sometimes called, make a variety of treats: pie, jam and jelly, upside-down cake with the French version of the English name "pouding," "grand-pères" (dumplings cooked in blueberry syrup), crêpes filled with stewed fruit, "parfaits" topped with blueberries, and cantaloupe melon filled with blueberries soaked in liqueur and decorated with blueberry-flavoured whipped cream.

MAURICIE-LANAUDIÈRE

Travelling the side roads of Lanaudière, I have the sense that, to be in harmony with the countryside, I should be in a horse-and-buggy. These tranquil farms and 17th century fieldstone farmhouses date back to the earliest seigneurial period. A covered bridge over the slow-flowing Bayonne River is no surprise; modern silos jolt the visitor's imagination back to the present. This lush farming country is called "green lowlands" by agricultural scientists, who give credit to the Champlain Sea that once, about 13,000 years ago, covered this plain. Every type of agricultural production seems to flourish here, including the newer specialty farms producing deer, wapiti, bison, lamb, rabbit, game birds, ostrich, emu, exceptional cheeses, and organic grains. Louiseville celebrates buckwheat, one of the earliest grains to be grown in Quebec, with an annual fall buckwheat pancake festival.

Talking of buckwheat with Micheline Mongrain-Dontigny, who has written cookbooks about the traditional recipes of the Mauricie and other regions of Quebec, she said she'll never make another tourtière, whatever the filling, without using buckwheat flour in her pie dough. (She suggests one-fifth buckwheat flour to four-fifths all-purpose.) "It gives so much better flavour to the meat."

Along the St. Lawrence River, where it widens into Lac Saint-Pierre is goose- and duck-hunting country and the popular fish are trout and perch. Far to the north, game hunting brings home deer, moose, hare, and partridge, all foods for the best "cipaille," "ragoût," and "tourtière." Talking to hunters, often as they held open their freezer doors to show me their autumn prizes, I was regularly told to keep the cooking of these wild meats simple so the delicate flavours can be appreciated. A wine marinade, a sprinkling of salt pork "lardons" (crisply fried strips), some fresh or salted herbs (for recipe see page 167), and gentle cooking are among methods they recommend for accenting these extra-lean meats. Never overcook them, they warned, because they are so lean and may dry out. The same tip should apply to ostrich and emu, launched in North America only in recent years. I've been served plenty of these ratites (as these walking birds are termed) so overcooked, they tasted like pot roast. To arguments over whether these big birds should be part of the Quebec scene, consider that the pheasant was brought to Canada from England and we have long enjoyed it. The jury is out.

If you're not a hunter, yet love the taste of these specialty meats, you'll find fine terrines and other good foods at La Maison Staner in Saint-Alphonse-Rodriguez, north of Rawdon. Driving through resort country, I still remember my surprise at sighting the elegant Staner shop. I loaded my cooler with such treats as boar with venison sauce, bison tourtière, and partridge terrine.

The tourtière up the Saint-Maurice River is often a fish pie, using either salmon or trout. Constance Nemey of La Tuque fills her tourtière with poached trout fillets, chopped green onion, and cream. "Our visitors from France consider it gastronomic," said Constance, who with her husband, André Perron, runs a B and B called La Maison Claire-Fontaine.

Tommy cod, the tiny fish that cause a rush to the ice each winter, appears in plenty of dishes each January. Micheline Mongrain-Dontigny recommends this fish for frying, or braising with vegetables into a "gibelotte," or using the tiny eggs of the little fish, combined with a regular egg, to make an herb-flavoured omelette. She describes this delicacy as a cross between an omelette and a crêpe.

Tommy cod season is an excuse to join the party at Sainte-Anne-de-la-Pérade, a town east of Trois-Rivières where the Sainte-Anne River flows into the St. Lawrence. The shore turns into a village of tiny fishing shacks, and amateurs are welcome to join in this easy sport. "The fish are hungry for the bait—little pieces of frozen pork liver. You'll catch plenty, but not so many as to interfere with beer-drinking," said a jovial regular. Perch is more prized by chefs in this region. Joël Zaetta, long-time chef at Chez Claude, the excellent restaurant in the Castel des Prés in Trois-Rivières-Ouest, makes it into a fish mousse or poaches it along with crayfish to serve with a chive-flavoured wine sauce.

SOUPE AUX TOMATES

Tomato soup

A Landmark Church

Berthierville, across the St. Lawrence from Sorel, is located on the one-time seigneury of Autray, which dates from 1637. The town is cited nowadays as the birthplace of the late racing car hero Gilles Villeneuve, who has a museum devoted to his career on the outskirts of town. But a little, whitewashed church called the Cuthbert Chapel is the treasured landmark. The first Protestant church in Quebec, it was built in 1786 by James Cuthbert, one of Gen. James Wolfe's officers, who acquired the seigneury in 1765 after Wolfe's conquest of the French on the Plains of Abraham in 1759. Now the centrepiece of a tranquil park not far from the 19th century main street, the chapel serves as a cultural centre. Nearby is one of Quebec's remaining covered bridges, this one built over the Bayonne River in 1883.

When Renée Désy Audette was growing up in Berthierville, her mother, Irene Plante Désy, would make a batch of this rosy red, onion-flavoured soup in the morning so it would mellow for the evening meal. Old-fashioned rolled oats provide the best flavour, says Mme Audette, who likes to add garlic for an extra tang.

> 1 tablespoon (15 mL) butter
> 1 small onion, chopped
> 2 cloves garlic, crushed
> 4 cups (1 L) chicken stock or water
> 2 cups (500 mL) peeled, chopped tomatoes, or
>   1 can (19 ounces/540 mL) canned tomatoes, chopped, with the juice
> 1 carrot, peeled and chopped
> ¼ cup (60 mL) old-fashioned rolled oats
> ¼ teaspoon (1 mL) dried thyme or basil
> 1 teaspoon (5 mL) granulated sugar
> Salt and ground black pepper

In a large, heavy saucepan, heat butter over medium heat and cook onion and garlic, stirring, for 2 minutes or until softened. Add chicken stock, tomatoes, carrot, rolled oats, thyme, and sugar; season with salt and pepper to taste. Bring to a boil. Reduce heat and simmer, partially covered, for 45 minutes. Serve in heated soup bowls.

Six servings

CRETONS

Quebec's traditional country pâté should mature for at least two days in the refrigerator before you serve it. This recipe belonged to the late Gilberte Morin Martinson of La Tuque. She liked to serve it sliced on a leaf of lettuce with pickles and tomatoes, and fresh, crusty bread.

1½ pounds (750 g) shoulder of pork
1 pork kidney, trimmed
2 small onions, chopped
1 clove garlic, minced
¼ teaspoon (1 mL) ground allspice
Salt and freshly ground pepper
1 cup (250 mL) water

Mauricie-Lanaudière Menu

Cretons (p. 121)
Potted pork

Medaillons de boeuf au Brie et aux noix (p. 124)
Beef medallions with Brie and walnuts
French fried potatoes
Braised carrots and broccoli

Crêpes Normandes (p. 134)
Pancakes, Norman style

Grind pork and pork kidney in a meat grinder or coarsely chop in food processor using on/off pulse. Place in a heavy saucepan with onions, garlic, allspice, and salt and pepper to taste. Add enough water to come ¾ of the way up the meat. Place over medium heat and cook, stirring, until mixture comes to a boil. Reduce heat and simmer gently for 2 hours.

Rinse small, individual bowls or a 1-quart (1 L) mould with cold water. If necessary, season meat with more salt and pepper to taste. Pour mixture into bowls or mould. Cool to room temperature, then cover and chill in refrigerator. For best flavour, refrigerate for 2 days before serving. Serve in slices or as a spread.

Makes about 4 cups (1 L)

TIP: May be refrigerated for up to 4 days or frozen up to 2 months.

CHAUDRÉE DE POISSON FRAIS DU LAC SAINT-PIERRE

Fresh fish chowder

Lumberjack Life

The hefty fare served in the era of lumbering along the Saint-Maurice River is recreated at the Village du Bûcheron, a model 19th century lumber camp at Grandes-Piles. Guides, some of them descendants of the wood cutters and draveurs who rode the logs down river, show some 30,000 annual visitors how the workers would cut trees and drag them out of the bush, saw logs, trim boards, and gather for sustaining meals. On the menu then and now: pea soup, ragoût, baked beans, pâté à la viande (the region's name for tourtière), fricas-séed potatoes, pickles, coleslaw, bread with molasses, and sugar pie. The menu names—Assiette du Jobber, Assiette du Chore Boy, and Assiette du Cook—in the village restaurant demonstrate the mixture of English and French used in the camps, which were often owned by English businessmen. Recipes for the traditional fare come from families in the area and the food is

At Auberge du Lac Saint-Pierre, Chef Patrice Lafrenière likes to use perch and crayfish, favourites on his lake. This lusty soup is a meal-in-one at lunch or supper. Fish may be replaced with other varieties of white fish. Shrimp may replace crayfish. Serve it with crusty bread and a green salad.

> 1 pound (500 g) fillets of fresh doré (walleye)
> ½ pound (250 g) perch fillets
> ¼ pound (125 g) whitefish fillets
> 8 cups (2 L) fish stock
> 12 crayfish or large shrimp
> 2 tablespoons (30 mL) butter, softened
> 2 tablespoons (30 mL) all-purpose flour
> ⅓ cup (75 mL) whipping cream
> ¾ cup (175 mL) white wine
> 3 medium leeks, white part only, chopped
> 3 medium potatoes, peeled, cubed
> 1 stalk celery, diced
> 1 carrot, diced
> 1 small zucchini, diced

Remove any bones in fish and cut fillets in 1-inch (2.5 cm) pieces. Place fish stock in a large saucepan and bring to a boil. Reduce heat to medium–low. Add fish pieces and poach until opaque; do not overcook. Remove with slotted spoon; place in a bowl and cover. Add crayfish to simmering stock and cook just until pink. Remove with slotted spoon; remove shells from crayfish and discard shells. Place crayfish in bowl with fish. Meanwhile, bring fish stock to a boil over high heat and reduce by half. In a bowl, blend butter and flour to form a paste and whisk into stock; add cream and simmer for 5 minutes, stirring occasionally, until slightly thickened. Set aside.

In a small stainless steel saucepan, bring wine to a boil and add leeks; reduce to medium heat and cook for 5 minutes or until tender. Add to soup mixture. Bring a medium saucepan of water to a boil and cook potatoes, celery, and carrot for 6 to 8 minutes or until just tender. Add zucchini for the final minute. Drain, then add to soup. When ready to serve, heat soup until piping hot; add reserved fish mixture and gently reheat. Season to taste with salt and pepper. Serve at once.

Eight servings

TIP: The fish and crayfish may be cooked, the soup mixture prepared, and the vegetables cooked and added to the soup several hours in advance and refrigerated. Reheat soup and add fish and crayfish just before serving.

good, and certainly sustaining. The camp has about 25 log buildings, including La Limerie, where saws were sharpened, La Cache, where provisions were protected from bears by an armed guard, and La Cookerie, ruled over by the cook, the most powerful man in the camp. There's a display of scale models of the various boats used in logging on the river in the century from 1850 to 1950; the last log runs ended only in 1996. The village is open from May 1 to Oct. 15. For information, call (819) 538-7895 or visit www.villagebucheron.qc.ca.

MEDAILLONS DE BOEUF
AU BRIE ET AUX NOIX

Beef medallions with Brie and walnuts

Chef Patrick Gérôme enlivens a simple beef steak with cheese, nuts, and herbs in this easy recipe from Auberge Le Baluchon in Saint-Paulin. The French fried potatoes he suggests with it could be replaced with baked or mashed potatoes.

Sauce
    ½ cup (125 mL) red wine
    1 large shallot, minced
    1 teaspoon (5 mL) black peppercorns, crushed
    ½ teaspoon (2 mL) dried thyme
    2 teaspoons (10 mL) tomato paste
    1 cup (250 mL) veal stock

In a medium, heavy stainless steel saucepan, combine wine, shallot, and crushed peppercorns; boil until reduced by half. Add thyme, tomato paste, and veal stock; bring to a boil. Simmer 5 minutes. Strain sauce through a sieve and keep warm.

    2 tablespoons (30 mL) olive oil
    1 pound (500 g) beef sirloin tip, cut ¾ to 1 inch
      (2 to 2.5 cm) thick, in 4 portions
    Salt and freshly ground pepper
    2½ ounces (75 g) Brie cheese, rind removed
    ¼ cup (60 mL) walnuts

A Prime Minister's Home

Step into the childhood home of Sir Wilfrid Laurier, Canada's first French-speaking prime minister (1896 to 1911), and the life of the family of a prosperous land surveyor comes alive. A tiny 1870 red brick house in the town of Ville-des-Laurentides (also known by its original name of Saint-Lin) is an authentic recreation of gentler times. You can walk through the tiny, red-decorated parlour and see willow-pattern

In a large, heavy frying pan, heat oil over high heat. Sear beef on both sides and continue to cook until medium-rare. Season meat with salt and pepper. Spread Brie over meat and cook 1 to 2 minutes more or until just heated through. Pour sauce onto 4 heated serving plates. Place steaks on sauce and sprinkle with nuts. Serve with French fried potatoes and a green salad.

china in a corner cupboard, wool-spinning on a wheel, and candle-making on the kitchen table. The plants of the period are being grown in the little garden, there's an interpretation centre to this historic site, and both period animations and concerts are offered on summer weekends. A walking tour guide to the historic buildings in the town is available. For information call (450) 439-3702.

TIP: Sirloin may be replaced with 4 filets mignons, cut ¾ inch (2 cm) thick.

LE FILET DE SANGLIER
AUX HERBES DE PROVENCE

Herb-flavoured fillet of boar

The Hero Priests of Joliette

Père Fernand Lindsay is revered
around Joliette, particularly each
July when his creation, the annual
Festival International de Lanaudière,
takes place. The founder-director of
this celebrated musical event is
sometimes called the Curé Labelle
of Lanaudière, a reference to Curé
Antoine Labelle of Saint-Jérôme,
who helped colonize the
Laurentians over a century ago.
Père Lindsay is a serious gastronome, recognized in the better
restaurants of the region. But he
prefers to talk about the art treasures of the small but outstanding
Musée d'Art de Joliette, where you'll
find works by such Quebec artists
as Paul-Emile Borduas, Jean-Paul
Riopelle, Marc-Aurèle de Foy Suzor-
Côté, and Ozias Leduc, including
the latter's still life of red-skinned

Chef Patrick Gérôme of Auberge Le Baluchon obtains boar from
a game farm not far from Saint-Paulin. You may substitute pork
tenderloin in this quick-roasted dish, which has a little honey in the
sauce.

> 2 tablespoons (30 mL) Dijon mustard
> 2 teaspoons (10 mL) "herbes de Provence"*
> 1 tablespoon (15 mL) butter
> 1 tablespoon (15 mL) olive oil
> 2 boar fillets, about ½ pound (250 g) each, each
>   cut in half**
> ¼ cup (60 mL) fresh lemon juice
> ⅓ cup (75 mL) honey
> 1½ teaspoons (7 mL) black peppercorns,
>   coarsely ground

*This herb mixture may be replaced with a mixture of
thyme, savory, marjoram, and oregano.
**One pound (500 g) pork tenderloin may be substituted.
Prepare meat the same way, but roast for 25 to 30 minutes,
until temperature on a meat thermometer is 160°F (75°C).

In a small bowl, combine mustard and herbs. In a large, heavy frying pan, heat butter and oil over high heat and brown boar fillets on both sides. Remove pan from heat and spread boar with mustard mixture. Arrange in a shallow roasting pan and roast in preheated 350°F (180°C) oven for 8 to 10 minutes or until meat is medium-rare. Transfer to a warm serving platter and keep warm.

To make sauce, place roasting pan over medium heat; stir in lemon juice, honey, and peppercorns, and cook, stirring, for 2 minutes. Pour sauce over meat and serve with steamed, fresh vegetables.

Four servings

onions. Père Lindsay, a member of the order of the Clercs de Saint-Viateur, had an esteemed colleague in the late Père Wilfrid Corbeil, who launched the museum with a donation of the order's paintings and religious sculpture. Another Joliette location for exceptional art is the Cathedral of Saint-Charles-Borromée, where eight frescoes by Ozias Leduc decorate the walls. And there's a big collection of Leduc's religious frescoes in the Eglise Notre-Dame-de-la-Présentation in Shawinigan-Sud.

RÔTI DE PORC ET PATATES JAUNES

Roast pork with pan-browned potatoes

TIP: Up to 4 hours in advance, recipe may be prepared up to the point where pan is placed in the oven.

This cold weather combination of garlic-flavoured pork and pan-browned potatoes is a favourite in the Mauricie. Micheline Mongrain-Dontigny, author of a cookbook of traditional Mauricie recipes, considers this a Sunday dish.

1 loin of pork (3 pounds/1.5 kg)
3 cloves garlic, halved
1 piece pork rind, 3 ounces (90 g)
1 onion, sliced
Salt and freshly ground pepper
2 tablespoons (30 mL) butter, softened
1 tablespoon (15 mL) dry mustard
½ teaspoon (2 mL) dried marjoram
1 cup (250 mL) water
6 medium potatoes, peeled

Using a sharp-tipped knife, make 6 incisions in the roast and insert halves of garlic. Place pork rind in a shallow roasting pan. Arrange onion slices on rind and place roast on top. Season roast with salt and pepper to taste. Blend butter with mustard and brush lean parts of roast. Sprinkle with marjoram and pour water into bottom of pan. Roast, uncovered, for 1 hour at 350°F (180°C).

Arrange potatoes around roast. Continue roasting another 1½ hours, turning potatoes once during cooking, and basting meat every 15 minutes. (If pan juices evaporate during roasting, add a little more water.)

Transfer roast and potatoes to a heated serving platter. Skim fat from pan and transfer remaining juices to a gravyboat to serve with meat and potatoes.

Six servings

RAGOÛT DE POISSON DES CHENEAUX

When the catch of these tiny fish was good in January, the late Maria de Bellefeuille Letourneau of Trois-Rivières would make this layered fish and vegetable dish and cook it in her wood stove.

¼ pound (125 g) salt pork, diced, or 4 slices bacon, diced
2 to 3 pounds (1 to 1.5 kg) tommy cod or smelts
5 medium potatoes, peeled, thinly sliced
½ cup (125 mL) chopped fresh parsley
Salt and freshly ground white pepper
2 medium onions, thinly sliced
2 carrots, peeled, thinly sliced, blanched (optional)
3 cups (750 mL) water
Butter (optional)

In a large frying pan, cook salt pork over medium heat for 5 minutes or until crisp and reserve. Clean fish, removing heads and tails but not bones. In a heavy, 2-quart (2 L) casserole with a lid, layer ¼ of the potatoes in the bottom of the casserole. Top with ⅓ of the fish. Sprinkle with parsley, salt, and pepper to taste. Layer with ⅓ of the onions. Repeat layers twice more. Add carrots at this point. Top with final layer of potatoes. Pour water slowly and carefully into casserole. Sprinkle with salt pork and dot with butter. Cover and bake in preheated 375°F (190°C) oven for 40 minutes. Remove cover and bake for another 15 to 20 minutes until potatoes are tender and browned.

Six to eight servings

Cheese: A Specialty

Celebrating the cheese makers of Quebec is a shop in Vieux Terrebonne that sells only Quebec cheeses, as many as 150 of them. Called Fromagerie Arvin, the tiny store at 739 St. Pierre St. ([450] 492-8211) is the project of Denise DeCarufel-Archat, whose secret to success is the cheese maturing cellar she operates under the store. Some local cheeses are sold from nearby farms. Prize-winners include goat farms in Saint-Roch-de-l'Achigan-Chèvrerie Les Trois Clochettes and Fromagerie La Suisse Normande, and Fromagerie du Chemin du Roy in Lanoraie. Fromagerie du Champ à la Meule at Notre-Dame-de-Lourdes is known for Victor et Berthold, a washed-rind raw-milk cheese. The Conseil de développement bioalimentaire de Lanaudière publishes guides to cheese farms and other specialty producers. Call (450) 753-7486 or (800) 363-1726.

SUPREME D'OIE RÔTIE AUX POMMES

Roast goose breast with apples

Where to Stay

Auberge Le Baluchon, 3550 des Trembles Rd., Saint-Paulin, is an inn and spa built in quiet woodlands only 10 years ago. A prize-winner for its comfortable accommodation and light, regional cuisine, served in a lofty dining room by Chef Patrick Gérôme, who was named Quebec's chef of the year in 1999. Comfortable cabins surround the main buildings; expensive; (819) 268-2555, (800) 789-5968; www.baluchon.com. Nearby is the Seigneurie Volant, where tourists can visit a mill, forge, chapel, sugar shack, and the brewery Les Bières de la Nouvelle-France; (819) 268-5500.

Auberge du Lac Saint-Pierre, 1911 Notre-Dame St., Pointe-du-Lac, is a comfortable, modern inn on a promontory overlooking Lac Saint-Pierre, a wide stretch of the St. Lawrence River valued by hunters as a stopping-off place for

In goose- and duck-hunting country, it's natural that Chef Patrice Lafrenière of Auberge du Lac Saint-Pierre at Pointe-du-Lac specializes in these meats. He likes the new free-range goose that's being raised just across the St. Lawrence River at Baie-du-Febvre. Leaner and offering more flavour than the usual domestically raised goose, this meat pairs naturally with apples. Duck, available whole or cut up, may be substituted for goose.

> 1¼ pounds (625 g) goose breast or 4 duck breasts, skin on
> 1 tablespoon (15 mL) fat rendered from goose or duck, or olive oil
> 1 small shallot, chopped
> 2 red Cortland apples, not peeled, diced
> 1 tablespoon (15 mL) maple syrup
> ¼ cup (60 mL) maple or cider vinegar
> 2 tablespoons (30 mL) red wine
> 1½ cups (375 mL) goose, duck, or veal stock

Using a sharp knife, cut slits diagonally all over skin of goose or duck. Heat a heavy, cast-iron frying pan over high heat; sear meat on both sides, beginning skin-side down, until golden. Turn meat skin-side up.

Goose: Transfer pan to preheated 325°F (160°C) oven and roast for 5 to 6 minutes. Turn off oven with oven door ajar and leave meat in oven for another 10 minutes for medium-rare.

Duck: Transfer pan to oven preheated to 350°F (180°C) and roast for 5 minutes. Remove pan from oven and let stand, covered, at room temperature for 5 minutes for medium-rare.

In another frying pan, heat 1 tablespoon (15 mL) pan drippings, or oil, over medium heat. Cook shallot, stirring, for 2 minutes; add apples and maple syrup and cook, stir-ring, just until apples begin to soften. Add vinegar and wine and cook until reduced by half. Add the stock and boil until sauce is reduced and syrupy.

To serve, cut meat into diagonal slices and drizzle with sauce. Serve with boiled potatoes, browned briefly in hot goose fat or oil, or polenta. Add fresh, steamed vegetables in season.

Four servings

the snow goose and ducks and for sports fishing. Excellent regional cuisine, thanks to Chef Patrice Lafrenière; moderately priced; (819) 377-5971, (888) 377-5971; www.aubergelacst-pierre.com.

SOUFFLÉ AUX NAVETS

Turnip soufflé

Walk into History

The cast-iron stoves that changed
cooking and heating practices
throughout New France were made
at Canada's first company town, the
ironworks called Forges-du-Saint-
Maurice (photo opposite), started in
1730 north of Trois-Rivières. Now a
national historic site, the ironworks
includes the restored ironmaster's
house, museum, sound-and-light
show about settlement life, the blast
furnace and forges, and an exhibit
of kitchen equipment of each period
the forge operated, until 1883.
Bilingual, costumed guides bring
the unusual settlement to life. Exit
191 off highway 55 north onto St.
Michel Blvd. Open May 8 to
Oct.15. Admission. Call (819) 378-
5116. The one-time trading post of
Trois-Rivières, founded in 1634, has
an historic walk along Ursulines St.
Some 17th and 18th century buildings stage art exhibitions; the 1697
Ursulines' convent has a museum
displaying sculpture, silver, wood-
carving, embroidery, and painting.

Turnips, or rutabaga as the big yellow roots are often called, are a
year-round basic throughout Quebec. Shirley Rousseau of Trois-
Rivières makes this inexpensive vegetable dish to serve with
roasted or cold meats and a green vegetable or salad.

> 6 cups (1.5 L) peeled, cubed turnips
> ¼ cup (60 mL) butter, melted
> 2 eggs, beaten
> 3 tablespoons (45 mL) all-purpose flour
> 1 tablespoon (15 mL) brown sugar
> 1 teaspoon (5 mL) baking powder
> ¾ teaspoon (4 mL) salt
> Pinch freshly ground pepper
> Pinch nutmeg
> ⅓ cup (75 mL) fine, dry bread crumbs

In a saucepan of boiling, salted water, cook turnips until
tender. Drain; mash until smooth. Blend in 2 tablespoons
(30 mL) of the melted butter and the beaten eggs. In a
bowl, combine flour, brown sugar, baking powder, salt,
pepper, and nutmeg. Add dry ingredients to turnip mixture and mix well. Spread mixture in a buttered 2-quart
(2 L) baking dish. In a bowl, combine bread crumbs and
remaining melted butter; sprinkle over the turnips. Bake in
a preheated 375°F (190°C) oven for 25 to 30 minutes or
until golden brown.

Six servings

TIP: Combining turnips with melted butter and beaten
eggs may be done the day before and the mixture refrigerated, covered. Allow 5 to 10 minutes extra baking time.

ASPERGES MARINÉES

Asparagus salad

Asparagus is the vegetable of choice in Mauricie and its popularity grows year by year. Suzanne Jobin of Trois-Rivières likes to cook the spears and marinate them in a garlic-flavoured vinaigrette. The same recipe may be used with artichokes or green beans.

2 tablespoons (30 mL) cider vinegar
2 cloves garlic, finely chopped
1 teaspoon (5 mL) dried oregano
½ teaspoon (2 mL) salt
¼ teaspoon (1 mL) freshly ground pepper
¼ teaspoon (1 mL) dry mustard
⅓ cup (75 mL) olive oil
18 to 20 spears (1 pound/500 g) fresh asparagus, trimmed
Lettuce

In a small bowl, combine vinegar, garlic, oregano, salt, pepper, and mustard. Whisk in oil in a stream, blending well. Place asparagus in a large deep frying pan and add ½ inch (1 cm) of water to pan. Place over high heat and bring water to a boil; cover and cook for about 3 minutes or until asparagus is tender; do not overcook. Drain well; transfer to serving dish. Pour dressing over warm asparagus, cover and refrigerate for 2 to 3 hours, turning asparagus occasionally in marinade. To serve, arrange lettuce on 4 salad plates and top with asparagus.

Four servings

CRÊPES NORMANDES

Pancakes, Norman style

The paper-thin pancakes of Normandy and Brittany were end-lessly varied in the early days of New France. They would frequently be made of buckwheat flour and, when food was scarce, often made a meal. The crêpes would be fried in lard and served with molasses. This recipe from Adrienne Cloutier of La Tuque is a deluxe version calling for plenty of butter and rum.

> ¾ cup (175 mL) all-purpose flour
> 1 tablespoon (15 mL) granulated sugar
> ¼ teaspoon (1 mL) salt
> 2 cups (500 mL) milk
> 2 eggs, beaten
> Melted butter
> Rum Sauce (recipe follows)
> ¼ cup (60 mL) dark rum

In a bowl, combine flour, sugar, and salt. Using a whisk, beat in milk and eggs to make a very smooth batter. Strain batter through a fine sieve and let stand, covered, at room temperature for 1 hour.

Heat an 8-inch (20 cm) crêpe pan and lightly brush pan with melted butter. Pour a scant 3 tablespoons (45 mL) of batter into pan, tilting pan quickly to spread batter evenly. Cook crêpes until golden, but not browned, about 1 minute per side. Repeat until all the crêpes are cooked (about 18 in all), stacking them on a platter between pieces of waxed paper to prevent them from sticking together. To serve, fold the crêpes into quarters. Arrange on an ovenproof serving plate, cover loosely with aluminum foil, and reheat in a 350°F (180°C) oven for 15 to 20 minutes. Pour hot Rum Sauce over warmed crêpes and bring dish to the table. Heat the ¼ cup (60 mL) rum in another small saucepan, pour over crêpes and flame.

Six servings

Rum Sauce

⅓ cup (75 mL) butter
½ cup (125 mL) instant dissolving sugar
1 tablespoon (15 mL) lemon juice
¼ cup (60 mL) dark rum

Just before serving, combine butter and sugar in a saucepan. Place over medium heat; boil for 1 minute or until sugar is dissolved. Stir in lemon juice and rum. Serve hot.

TIP: Make crêpes several hours in advance, cover and refrigerate, then reheat.

BISCUITS AU GRUAU

Oatmeal lace cookies

Rolled oats linked with a sweet syrup make these cookies crisp and light. Originally a Scottish recipe, this version is adapted from one belonging to Mrs. George Matte of La Tuque. It's one of the British recipes in a French-language cookbook published by the churchwomen's group Le Cercle AFEAS de St. Zéphirin de la Tuque.

½ cup (125 mL) old-fashioned rolled oats
½ cup (125 mL) all-purpose flour
½ cup (125 mL) granulated sugar
¼ teaspoon (1 mL) baking powder
½ teaspoon (2 mL) ground ginger
⅓ cup (75 mL) melted butter
2 tablespoons (30 mL) corn syrup
2 tablespoons (30 mL) whipping cream
2 teaspoons (10 mL) vanilla extract

In a bowl, combine rolled oats, flour, sugar, baking powder, and ginger. Stir in butter, corn syrup, cream, and vanilla, mixing well. Using a 1 teaspoon (5 mL) measuring spoon, drop dough onto ungreased baking sheets, 4 inches (10 cm) apart. Bake in a preheated 375°F (190°C) oven for 6 to 8 minutes or until lightly browned. Let stand for a few seconds until firm enough to remove from baking sheets. Cool on rack.

Makes about 6 dozen 2-inch (5 cm) cookies

For a Perfect Picnic

The richest architectural heritage in the region is in Vieux Terrebonne, the old section of the bustling town of Terrebonne. Its park on the shores of the Rivière des Mille Îles, called Île des Moulins, is a sylvan spot that's ideal for a picnic, and includes ducks for the watching. Five restored 19th century buildings are linked to fur-trading baron Simon McTavish, who headed the North West Company and bought the seigneury in 1802. A flour mill, bakery, woollen textile mill, saw mill, and historic vegetable garden are explained by costumed guides, and historical plays are presented on the riverbank. If gastronomy is preferred, it's as close as Restaurant à l'Etang des Moulins, located in a restored greystone facing the old mills. Chef-proprietor Jean Cayer fled downtown Montreal years ago and his customers followed.

LAURENTIANS-OUTAOUAIS

When Curé Antoine Labelle came to call, so Laurentian legend has it, the huge 19th century priest was likely to linger over a meal for five or six hours, preaching his vision of settlements throughout the mountains. Today, this booming resort area is home to many who emulate Labelle's convivial tastes. Sainte-Adèle has some of the best restaurants and food stores in the province, stocked to satisfy the crowds that pour north from Montreal each weekend and an increasing number who live "up north" and commute south daily. Perched on a cliff on the highway is a giant Société des Alcools store with an impressive selection of wines, including 200 kinds of port. It's rivaled by equally big liquor stores in Saint-Sauveur and Saint-Jovite. Not far away at Sainte-Marguerite is a restaurant with a world-famous wine cellar—Bistro à Champlain. Sainte-Adèle has an exceptional supermarket run by the Chèvrefils family, offering luxury cuts of meat, a lavish fresh fish counter, and big variety of specialty fresh and packaged foods. The Bourassa food warehouse, decorated with a maroon wild west facade, allows the public to shop alongside chefs, even providing coats for the cheese cooler. The Sainte-Agathe bakery, La Huche à Pain, makes a traditional French country loaf called "capou" that sells throughout the region. La Chocolaterie Marie-Claude encourages visitors to enjoy their truffles or florentines on the spot with coffee. Capping off this centre for gastronomy from its mountaintop location is one of Quebec's finest training schools for chefs and wine stewards, École hotelière des Laurentides, feeding the demand for staff from fine dining establishments all over the region.

Chefs in the Laurentians used to have to import their food from Montreal. Now, say leading chefs such as Anne Desjardins of L'Eau à la Bouche in Sainte-Adèle and Val-David veteran Marcel Kretz, the only Canadian chef to be named to the Order of Canada, most of the specialties they like to cook are being produced a mere half-hour's drive away. Foods such as baby vegetables and edible flowers come from Pierre-André Daignault's Les Jardiniers du Chef at Blainville; chrysanthemum leaves and tiny bok choy from Terry Hussey's Les Jardins Insalada at Prévost. Game meats are plentiful from bird and deer farms in the region. Wild food foragers supply chefs with fiddleheads and mushrooms, while Gérald Le Gal, who runs Gourmet Sauvage in Sainte-Adèle, harvests and bottles about 60 delicacies, including milkweed relish, marinated cattail hearts, ox-eye daisy capers, and cloudberry jam. There are now so many specialty food and beverage producers in the Laurentians that they have launched a "table de concertation," a joint effort to help each other promote and sell their products.

Travelling northwest of Montreal, up the Mille Îles and Ottawa rivers, is a more tranquil experience. You pass the prosperous apple area of Oka and the Trappist monastery where the monks still sell the cheese their order launched over a century ago. (A dairy cooperative now makes the cheese; the "classic" Oka is closest to the original.) Fertile farms produce goat cheese, honey, wine, and pork. Boucannerie Belle-Rivière in Sainte-Scholastique smokes the kind of ham old-timers remember with smiles. On up the Ottawa is a rabbit farm, more honey makers, and one of Quebec's top goat cheese producers, La Ferme Foralpe, at Papineauville.

Contrasts in home cooking are distinct. In the Laurentians, old family recipes are economical—potatoes made into pies, celery leaves used as seasoning, buckwheat a favourite grain. The late Fleur-Ange Vanier Rochon, a descendant of two of Saint-Jovite's founding families, remembered her grandparents talking of the poor land they found. "Often nothing would grow. They would dig and find only sand and rocks," she told me. Along the Ottawa River, lusty lumberjack dishes turn up in old recipe collections, inherited from the era of the big log runs. French chefs have brought a lighter touch to the Outaouais. Yet just north of Hull, in the resort area called the Gatineau, Les Fougères, a fine regional restaurant at Chelsea, does a bustling business in robust cassoulets and tourtières to take out. Three tourtière versions are Nunavut caribou, lamb with red peppers and goat cheese, and duck mixed with pork and flavoured with orange and maple syrup.

CHAMPIGNONS MARINÉS ET FROMAGE DE CHÈVRE

Marinated mushrooms with goat cheese

Chef Charles Part likes to use a variety of mushrooms at Les Fougères, a country restaurant in Chelsea, north of Hull.

2 tablespoons (30 mL) butter
¼ cup (60 mL) extra–virgin olive oil
1 pound (500 g) portobello mushrooms, sliced
½ pound (250 g) white mushrooms, sliced
2 cloves garlic, finely chopped
1 lemon
2 red onions, minced
½ cup (125 mL) balsamic vinegar
½ cup (125 mL) Madeira or dry sherry
1 teaspoon (5 mL) whole dried coriander seeds
1 teaspoon (5 mL) fresh thyme leaves
1 teaspoon (5 mL) fresh tarragon leaves
4 ounces (125 g) fresh goat cheese, crumbled

In a large, heavy frying pan, heat butter and 2 tablespoons (30 mL) of the oil until sizzling; add mushrooms and garlic and cook, stirring, for 5 minutes or until mushrooms are softened. Cut peel from lemon and cut into fine strips. Squeeze juice from half the lemon; set peel and juice aside. Strain mushroom mixture, then pour mushroom juice back into pan. Add onions, vinegar, Madeira, lemon juice, and coriander; bring to a boil and cook for 5 minutes or until reduced by half. Stir in thyme and tarragon; remove from heat. Spoon mushrooms onto 4 warm serving plates, pour sauce over and sprinkle with cheese. Trim with lemon peel and oil.

Four servings

FOIE GRAS DE CANARD SAUCE HYDROMEL

Duck foie gras with Laurentian honey wine sauce

Chef Anne Desjardins of the celebrated restaurant L'Eau à la Bouche in Sainte-Adèle obtains her duck foie gras from Ferme des Becs-Fins in Saint-Canut and her honey products from InterMiel in Saint-Benoît. The two flavours complement each other, she believes.

> 1 teaspoon (5 mL) each black peppercorns, pink peppercorns, allspice, cardamom, and star anise
> ¼ cup (60 mL) honey wine, or mead
> ¼ cup (60 mL) honey vinegar or white wine vinegar
> ½ cup (125 mL) liquid honey
> 10 ounces (300 g) cooked, fresh duck foie gras*
> 3 to 4 cups (750 mL to 1 L) baby salad greens
> Freshly ground pepper

*Ready–made terrine of foie gras may be substituted. One reliable brand is made by the Quebec company Élevages du Périgord. It's sold in jars holding 125 grams (4 ounces), 190 grams (6.7 ounces), and 450 grams (1 pound). Warm jar just slightly in a pan of warm water and terrine will slip out easily.

Honey Explained

How bees do their work and the sweet results are explained at InterMiel, a large honey farm north of Oka, where you can take a tour to see every aspect of the honey business, including how some of the farm's 2,000 beehives are opened and the honey collected, why different kinds of honeys taste dissimilar, and how honey wine, or mead, is made. It's a project of two former Montreal schoolteachers, Christian and Viviane Macle, who run the farm and sell every conceivable honey product, including

Using a mortar and pestle or pepper grinder, crush black and pink peppercorns, allspice, cardamom, and star anise. Remove ½ teaspoon (2 mL) of the mixed spices and reserve. In a small stainless steel saucepan, bring honey wine and vinegar to a boil. Remove from heat and add larger amount of ground spice mixture. Let stand at least 10 minutes, then strain through a fine sieve and set liquid aside. In the saucepan, bring honey to a boil over medium heat and cook until caramel–coloured. Remove from heat and stir in strained honey wine mixture and remaining ½ teaspoon (2 mL) ground spices.

Arrange 2 slices (about 2 ounces/50 grams) of foie gras on each of 6 serving plates. Surround with salad greens and drizzle with spiced honey syrup. Season with pepper and serve.

Six servings

TIP: Honey syrup will keep, covered, in the refrigerator, for up to a month.

coloured beeswax out of which candles are made. 10291 de La Fresnière, Saint-Benoit (Mirabel), exit 8 off highway 640 west. (800) 265-MIEL; www.intermiel.com.

POTAGE AUX GOURGANES

Puréed bean soup

Chef Leopold Handfield, of Restaurant La Table Enchantée at Saint-Jovite, specializes in contemporary versions of traditional recipes. He serves his deluxe version of the gourgane bean soup of the Saguenay-Lac Saint-Jean and Charlevoix regions, flavouring it with vegetables and ham stock. A topping of whipped cream, browned under the broiler, is his final touch.

1 tablespoon (15 mL) butter
1 carrot, cubed
1 onion, chopped
½ cup (125 mL) peeled, cubed potatoes
¼ cup (60 mL) cubed rutabaga
5 cups (1.25 L) ham stock
2 cups (500 mL) shelled gourgane beans*
Salt and freshly ground pepper
⅔ cup (150 mL) whipping cream

*Fresh gourgane beans are best, but frozen gourgane or fava beans may be substituted.

In a large, heavy saucepan, heat butter over medium heat and cook carrot, onion, potatoes, and rutabaga, stirring often, for 10 minutes. Add ham stock (or water and a ham bone) and bring to a boil. Add gourgane beans, reduce heat to medium-low, and simmer, partly covered, for about 2 hours or until beans are tender. (If using a ham bone, remove it at this point.) Purée soup in a blender or food processor until smooth. Season with salt and pepper to taste.

In a bowl, whip cream until stiff peaks form. Pour hot soup into 4 ovenproof bowls (such as the type used for onion soup). Top with a generous spoonful of whipped cream and place under a hot broiler just until cream is lightly browned. Serve at once.

Four servings

TIP: Once puréed and seasoned, soup may be refrigerated for up to 6 hours.

CRÈME DE BETTERAVES LA SEIGNEURIE AUX ÉPICES ET AU MIEL DE TRÈFLE

Curried beet soup with chives

Laurentians-Outaouais Menu

Foie gras de canard sauce
hydromel (p.140)
*Duck foie gras with Laurentian
honey wine sauce*

Crème de betteraves La Seigneurie
aux épices et au miel de trèfle
(p. 144)
Curried beet soup with chives

Tourtière de Fleur-Ange (p. 148)
Fleur-Ange's pork pie
Green salad with chopped
mushrooms

Soupe au melon (p. 156)
Melon soup

When Marcel Mundel was chef at Château Montebello on the Ottawa River, he made this soup by cooking onions, beets, and potatoes together slowly, and then adding to their natural sweetness with a touch of curry and honey. This soup, served by the Alsace-born chef to a group of food writers at a 1995 Cuisine Canada conference at the hotel, is a favourite.

2 tablespoons (30 mL) butter
1 onion, chopped
3 cups (750 mL) peeled, cubed beets
2 cups (500 mL) peeled, cubed potatoes
2 to 3 teaspoons (10 to 15 mL) curry paste
 or powder
6 cups (1.5 L) chicken or vegetable stock
1 to 2 tablespoons (15 to 30 mL) honey
Salt and freshly ground pepper
½ cup (125 mL) whipping cream, whipped
 (optional)
Chopped fresh chives

In a large saucepan, melt butter over medium heat. Add onion and cook for 3 minutes to soften. Add beets, potatoes, and curry powder. Cover and cook over medium-low heat, stirring occasionally, for 15 minutes or until vegetables are softened. Add stock and simmer for 25 minutes or

until vegetables are very tender. Purée soup in batches in a
blender or food processor until very smooth. Return to
saucepan, and season with honey, salt, and pepper to taste.
Add more stock to thin soup, if necessary. Reheat until
piping hot and ladle into warmed soup bowls. Spoon a
dollop of whipped cream on top of each serving, and
sprinkle with chives.

Six servings

TARTE CHAUDE AU FROMAGE DE CHÈVRE

Goat cheese tart

Chef Anne Desjardins (photo opposite) uses local goat cheese and wild mushrooms in this appetizer from her menu at L'Eau à la Bouche, a Sainte-Adèle restaurant that's been named one of Quebec's best.

> 1 deep 9–inch (23 cm) pie shell, lined with pastry (recipe p. 15)

> 1 tablespoon (15 mL) butter
> ½ pound (250 g) sliced mushrooms
> 7 ounces (200 g) cooked ham, diced
> 7 ounces (200 g) fresh goat cheese
> 3 eggs
> 1 cup (250 mL) whipping cream
> 1 small clove garlic, finely chopped
> 1 shallot, finely chopped
> 2 teaspoons (10 mL) finely chopped fresh savory, or 1 teaspoon (5 mL) dried
> Salt and freshly ground pepper

Cover pie shell with aluminum foil; add dry peas or beans so pastry holds its shape while baking. Bake in a preheated 375°F (190°C) oven for 10 minutes. Remove peas and foil and set pastry shell aside. In a large, heavy frying pan, heat

The Picnic Tradition

The Indians, first inhabitants of Quebec, are believed to have taught the French settlers to cook and eat outdoors when the weather was fine, a custom unheard of at the time in France. The spring "sugaring off" maple syrup feast in the woods, the fish fry on the beach, and the late summer corn boil, "épluchette de blé d'inde," are examples of their teaching. The pleasure of eating corn was another Indian lesson. When Anne Desjardins, chef-proprietor of the Sainte-Adèle hotel-restaurant L'Eau à la Bouche, served tender, buttered kernels of fresh corn to a group of chefs from France, she found her visitors puzzled. They left the corn on their plates because, she reasoned, in France this vegetable is considered fit only for animals.

butter over medium heat and cook mushrooms for 3 minutes or just until they release their liquid and begin to brown. Layer into pie shell. Sprinkle ham over mushrooms. Place cheese in a bowl. Using an electric beater, beat in eggs, one at a time; beat in cream, garlic, shallot, and savory. Season with salt and pepper to taste. Pour egg mixture into pie shell, lifting mushrooms and ham gently with a fork so ingredients are combined. Bake in preheated 375°F (190°C) oven for about 30 minutes or until filling is set and top is lightly browned. Let stand 15 minutes before serving.

Six servings

TIP: Pie shell may be baked in advance.

TOURTIÈRE DE FLEUR-ANGE

Fleur-Ange's pork pie

Le Roi du Nord

The wilderness that was the Laurentian region was colonized in the late 19th century because of a priest who can be called one of Quebec's earliest land developers—Curé Antoine Labelle of Saint-Jérôme. His name can be found on a highway, a town, a lake, and a county. Concerned about the flood of French Canadians moving to work in New England factories, he dreamt of settling the entire region from Montreal to Winnipeg and Hudson's Bay with French Catholics, "to conquer our conquerors," as he put it. The forceful curé pressured the Quebec government to pass the "100 acres bill," which gave any family with 12 living children crown land in the north. Then he pushed builders to make roads and extend the railway into the mountains. Called "the king of the north," he was credited with persuading about 5,000 to go in search of "les terres en bois debout" (free land with timber still standing), which resulted in the founding of 20 new parishes.

Alsace-born Marcel Kretz of Val David, named to the Order of Canada for his role in training young chefs to compete at home and abroad, says the traditional pork pie of his late mother-in-law, Fleur-Ange Vanier Rochon, is the best he's ever eaten. Mme Rochon used pork in her meat mixture, and seasoned the pie with celery and savory.

2 pounds (1 kg) lean ground pork
1 cup (250 mL) water
1 cup (250 mL) chopped celery
½ cup (125 mL) chopped celery leaves
2 large onions, chopped
2 cloves garlic, chopped
½ cup (125 mL) chopped fresh parsley
1 tablespoon (15 mL) chopped fresh savory or
  1 teaspoon (5 mL) dried
Pinch each ground cinnamon and cloves
Salt and freshly ground pepper
Pastry for 2 double-crust, 8-inch (20 cm) pies
  (recipe p. 15)
1 egg yolk beaten with 1 tablespoon (15 mL) milk

In a large, heavy saucepan over medium heat, combine pork, water, celery and leaves, onions, garlic, parsley, savory, cinnamon, cloves, and salt and pepper to taste. Cook, stirring occasionally, for 30 minutes, adding more water, if necessary, to prevent mixture from drying. Adjust seasonings, if necessary. Let cool.

Line two 8-inch (20 cm) pie plates with pastry and fill with meat mixture. Roll out top crusts, cutting a generous vent in the centre of each. (Mme Rochon always cut her vents in the shape of an evergreen tree.) Cover each pie with top crust, trim pastry, crimp the edges to seal, and cut small steam vents. Brush top of pastry with egg yolk and milk mixture.

Bake pies in a preheated 400°F (200°C) oven for 35 to 40 minutes or until crust is golden. Serve either hot or cold with pickles or relish.

Twelve to sixteen servings

TIP: Meat mixture may be made ahead and refrigerated. Unbaked pies may be refrigerated for 24 hours, or frozen. Thaw in refrigerator before baking.

FOIE DE PORC AU BACON SAUCE DE THÉ

Pork liver and bacon with tea sauce

In Quebec's early days, the pot of tea on the back of the stove came into play when gravy was being made. Montreal chef Richard Bergeron remembers his grandmother, Alphonsine Lemieux Bergeron, serving this dish at restaurants she ran in La Minerve, north of Mont Tremblant.

8 slices maple-smoked bacon
3 tablespoons (45 mL) all-purpose flour
Salt and freshly ground pepper
1 pound (500 g) pork liver*, cut in ½-inch
  (1 cm) slices
2 tablespoons (30 mL) browned flour**
1½ cups (375 mL) strong, cold tea
Chopped fresh parsley

*Calves' liver or beef liver may be substituted.
**Sprinkle flour in heavy frying pan and cook, stirring, over medium heat just until flour turns the colour of brown sugar, about 5 minutes. Or use a commercial brand.

In a large, heavy frying pan, cook bacon until crisp. Transfer to heated serving platter and keep warm in a low oven. Strain bacon fat through a fine sieve and return to pan. Place flour on a plate and season with salt and pepper to taste; coat liver slices with seasoned flour, shaking to remove excess.

Heat frying pan over medium-high heat and sear liver on both sides. Reduce heat and continue cooking to desired degree of doneness, keeping inside of slices pink. Transfer liver to platter with bacon and keep warm.

Sprinkle browned flour over pan drippings and cook, stirring, until bubbly. Add cold tea and simmer, stirring, until mixture turns a rich, medium brown and sauce has reduced and thickened. Season with salt and pepper to taste, strain through a fine sieve, and serve over liver. Sprinkle liver with parsley and serve with bacon.

Four servings

TIP: Vegetable oil may be substituted for bacon fat.

PERDIX À LA FAÇON DE MON GRAND-PÈRE RAOUL

Grandfather's partridge

A Unique Seigneury

Tucked away on the shore of the Ottawa River, next to the 1930 sprawling log hotel now called Château Montebello, is the elegant, turreted 1850 manor house of Louis-Joseph Papineau, speaker in Lower Canada's House of Assembly and leader of the Patriotes in the 1837 rebellion. Papineau built the turreted stone mansion on his family's seigneury, called La Petite Nation, which originally extended north into wilderness that is now the site of the hotel's golf course and Kenauk nature reserve. Under restoration and furnished in Victorian style, this national historic site is open to the public from May to October. The little stone Papineau chapel displays the 1837 rebellion flag. For information, call (819) 423-6965 or visit www.parcscanada.gc.ca/papineau.

Robert Bourassa, chef-owner of Café Henry Burger, the restaurant near the National Museum of Civilization in Hull, remembers his grandmother preparing her mother's recipe for the traditional Quebec dish of braised partridge and cabbage. She would cook the birds that his grandfather, at one time the president of the Montreal food company La Belle Fermière, would shoot on the grounds of the Seignory Club, now Château Montebello. Bourrassa has created this refined version of his family recipe. He serves it with cubed carrots, turnips, potatoes, and sliced zucchini, steaming the vegetables and then sautéing them briefly in a little butter. Recommended wine: an Alsatian white Gewürztraminer or a red Bordeaux Côte-du-Bourg.

2 partridges (about 1 pound/500 g each)
2 tablespoons (30 mL) white, unsalted pork fat,
  cut into thin strips
½ cup (125 mL) chicken stock
½ cup (125 mL) lean salt pork, cut in thin strips,
  or 2 tablespoons (30 mL) vegetable oil
2 Spanish onions, minced
½ medium red cabbage, finely chopped
2 apples, peeled, coarsely chopped
1 teaspoon (5 mL) chopped, fresh thyme, or
  ½ teaspoon (2 mL) dried
1 clove garlic, chopped
2 tablespoons (30 mL) brown sugar
Salt and freshly ground pepper
2 pork sausages

To prevent partridge breasts from drying out, cut tiny slits in meat and insert strips of unsalted pork fat, using tip of a knife or a butcher's larding needle.

Truss birds by tying legs and wings with string. Place in a roasting pan and pour in chicken stock. Roast, uncovered, in a 325°F (160°C) oven for 30 to 45 minutes, or until meat is half-cooked, basting occasionally with stock. Let meat cool slightly and debone, keeping the larger pieces of meat intact. Refrigerate meat.

Place bones and pan drippings in a large heavy saucepan; add cold water to cover. Place over high heat and bring to a boil; reduce heat and simmer for 1 hour. Strain stock through a sieve and reserve. Place salt pork strips in a heavy, flameproof, 3-quart (3 L) casserole with a cover and cook over medium heat until lightly browned. (If preferred, replace pork drippings with vegetable oil.) Add onions, cabbage, and apples; cook, stirring, for 2 minutes. Cover casserole and bake in a 300°F (150°C) oven for 1 hour, adding a little partridge stock if mixture dries out.

Add partridge meat, thyme, garlic, brown sugar, and salt and pepper to taste. Pour 1 cup (250 mL) of the partridge stock over all and continue to bake, covered, for another hour. Add additional partridge stock if mixture begins to dry out. Remove cover for final 15 minutes of baking time. If desired, place casserole briefly under preheated broiler to brown partridge skin lightly.

Prick sausages all over with a fork. In a large frying pan, cook sausages over medium heat for 10 to 12 minutes, turning often, until browned and cooked through. Cut into diagonal slices and arrange around edges of casserole.

Four servings

TIP: Up to four hours in advance, recipe may be prepared and baked for 1 hour. Then the dish may be cooled, the partridge meat, other ingredients, and stock added, and the casserole refrigerated for 24 hours. Bring to room temperature and complete recipe.

FEUILLETES DES PETITS LEGUMES À LA CORIANDRE

Puff pastry with vegetables in coriander sauce

Guy Blain, chef-proprietor of L'Orée du Bois, a restaurant at Old Chelsea, north of Hull, obtains many of his fresh vegetables from local gardeners, and his wild mushrooms from nearby Gatineau Park. Blain's menu offers duck from both Brome Lake in Knowlton and Mariposa Farms in Plantagenet, Ontario. The chef, from Chateaudun in France's Loire district, smokes his own fish, flavours his own vinegars and oils, and grows herbs beside his comfortable, rustic restaurant.

Where to Stay

Inns and big hotels dot each lake and mountainside. For the finest food in a rustic but elegant restaurant, with a comfortable modern hotel nearby, L'Eau à la Bouche, member of the Paris-based Relais et Châteaux group of luxury establishments, is at 3003 Sainte-Adèle Blvd. (highway 117), north of Sainte-Adèle; (450) 229-2991, (888) 828-2991; expensive. Hôtel La Sapinière is a big hotel with a long history of good food and wine; 1244 de la Sapinière Rd., Val David; (819) 322-2020, (800) 567-6635; www.sapiniere.com; expensive. Château Montebello is a huge luxury resort with fine food; 392 Notre-Dame St. (highway 148), Montebello; (819) 423-6341, (800) 441-1414; www.cphotels.ca.

Coriander sauce

2 cups (500 mL) chicken stock
½ carrot, peeled
½ zucchini, peeled
1 small onion, cut into quarters
1 tablespoon (15 mL) dried coriander seeds, ground
¾ cup (175 mL) white wine
1 cup (250 mL) whipping cream

Combine chicken stock, carrot, zucchini, onion, and ground coriander in a stainless steel saucepan and cook, covered, over medium heat until vegetables are tender, about 30 minutes. Purée in a food processor or blender until very smooth. Set aside.

Add the wine to saucepan and boil, uncovered, until reduced by half. Add puréed stock mixture and cream. Bring to a boil and simmer, partially covered, until sauce thickens. Keep warm in covered saucepan over low heat.

Pastry

7 ounces (200 g) frozen puff pastry
1 egg yolk, lightly beaten

Roll out pastry to a 6 x 8 inch (15 x 20 cm) rectangle and cut into 6 individual rectangles, each 2 x 4 inches (5 x 10 cm) in size. Place pastry on a baking sheet, brush tops with egg yolk, and bake in a preheated 400°F (200°C) oven for 12 to 15 minutes, until puffed and golden. Split each pastry in half lengthwise and keep warm.

Vegetables

1 cup (250 mL) small cauliflower florets
1 small zucchini, cut into thin strips
1 red pepper, seeded and diced
1 small carrot, cut into thin strips
1 small parsnip, cut into thin strips
12 snow peas
6 Brussels sprouts, quartered
12 fiddleheads (optional)

In a pot of boiling, salted water, blanch each vegetable separately until tender-crisp; refresh each under cold water to chill. Drain well.

To serve, add vegetables to coriander sauce, and place over medium heat until piping hot. Place a pastry bottom on each of 6 serving plates. Spoon some of the vegetables and sauce onto each of the pastries and arrange the pastry halves on top. Serve immediately.

Six servings

TIP: Coriander sauce, pastry dough, and vegetables may each be prepared up to four hours in advance.

SOUPE AU MELON

Melon soup

Chef Anne Desjardins of L'Eau à la Bouche in Sainte-Adèle serves this fruit soup as a dessert when the cantaloupe melons are at their best.

Strawberry jelly

1½ teaspoons (7 mL) unflavoured gelatin
2 tablespoons (30 mL) cold water
1 cup (250 mL) fresh strawberries, or 1 package (300 g) frozen, unsweetened
3 tablespoons (45 mL) unpasteurized wild-flower honey
½ teaspoon (2 mL) chopped fresh gingerroot

In a small bowl, sprinkle gelatin over water and let stand to dissolve. In a blender, purée strawberries, honey, and ginger. Pour into a medium saucepan and heat to the boiling point. Remove from heat. Stir into gelatin mixture until smooth. Rinse a shallow pan with cold water, then pour in strawberry mixture. Refrigerate until firm.

Soup

1 ripe cantaloupe melon, peeled, cubed
1 cup (250 mL) honey wine (mead) or semi–sweet white wine
1 teaspoon (5 mL) grated fresh gingerroot
2 tablespoons (30 mL) wild-flower honey
1 tablespoon (15 mL) lemon juice

In a blender or food processor, purée melon, honey wine, ginger, honey, and lemon juice. Cover and refrigerate until cold.

Trimming

4 fresh strawberries, citronella mint leaves

To serve, chill 4 serving bowls. Cut strawberry jelly into 1½-inch (4 cm) squares and place in bowls. Pour in cantaloupe mixture. Decorate bowls with strawberries and mint leaves.

Four servings

TIP: Strawberry jelly may be made the day before, covered, and refrigerated. Soup may be prepared up to five hours in advance and refrigerated.

TARTE À LA FERLOUCHE

Molasses pie

Highway to the West

Along the Ottawa River road (highways 344 and 148), there's a British influence to the architecture, and the names of towns in the area—Grenville, Chatham, and Brownsburg—reveal their lineage. The river has been called the first trans-Canada highway, used first by fur traders, then in the 1830s and 1840s by the lumbering business, followed by steamers carrying both passengers and cargo. The British heritage is depicted in the Argenteuil museum. It's located in a handsome Georgian greystone that's been called the Carillon Barracks ever since it housed the British army in the 1837-38 rebellion of Lower Canada. Military uniforms, Victorian ice skates, toys, and wedding dresses, and a 19th century hand-operated fire pump are among the treasures on display; 50 Principale St., Carillon; (450) 537-3861.

This economical Quebec dessert was traditionally made with molasses. Recipes sometimes included maple syrup, cornstarch, and spices. Marie-Ange Rondeau of Buckingham, who taught cooking and ran a restaurant in her area for many years, makes her recipe for one of Quebec's favourite desserts with or without the raisins or other dried fruit. It's included in *Les recettes des fermières du Québec*, a collection of recipes the rural women's group published in 1978.

> 1 egg
> 1 cup (250 mL) molasses
> 1 cup (250 mL) raisins
> 1 tablespoon (15 mL) melted butter
> 3 tablespoons (45 mL) soft bread crumbs
> Juice of ½ lemon
> Pinch salt
> 1 8-inch (20 cm) pie shell, lined with pastry
> (see p. 15)

In a bowl, beat egg; stir in molasses, raisins, melted butter, bread crumbs, lemon juice, and salt. Pour into pastry-lined pie shell. Bake in a preheated 350°F (180°C) oven for 30 minutes or until filling is bubbling hot and lightly browned. Serve warm or at room temperature.

Six servings

TIP: Pie crust may be made up to 24 hours in advance.

GATEAU À LA CITROUILLE DE LOCHABER

Pumpkin cake

Pumpkins are a popular ingredient in cakes, cookies, pies, bread, and even soup, around Thurso, a lumbering town on the Ottawa River, which was originally settled by Scottish-Canadians. This recipe, named by its owner Florence Mongeon after her district, was included in a collection of recipes published by the local women's group Les Fermières de Thurso and called *Cent ans de tradition culinaire québécoise.*

TIP: Fresh pumpkin may be baked, then puréed and placed in 2-cup (500 mL) plastic containers and frozen to use for this cake, for soup, and for muffins.

3 cups (750 mL) all-purpose flour
2 teaspoons (10 mL) baking soda
2 teaspoons (10 mL) cinnamon
¾ teaspoon (4 mL) cloves
¼ teaspoon (1 mL) salt
½ cup (125 mL) shortening or butter
1¼ cups (300 mL) brown sugar
2 eggs
2 cups (500 mL) puréed pumpkin, or 1 can
    (19 ounces/540 mL) unsweetened pumpkin purée

In a bowl, combine flour, baking soda, cinnamon, ground cloves, and salt. In another bowl, cream shortening with brown sugar until fluffy; beat in eggs and pumpkin. Stir dry ingredients into creamed mixture to make a smooth batter.

Spread batter evenly in 2 greased 8½ x 4½-inch (1.5 L) loaf pans. Bake in a preheated 325°F (160°C) oven for 50 to 60 minutes or until tester inserted in centre comes out clean. Let cool in pans for 10 minutes, then turn out onto rack to cool completely.

Makes 2 loaf cakes

TARTE AU SUCRE

Fleur-Ange's sugar pie

Maple syrup has never been plentiful in the Laurentians. More frequently, families served a pie with a brown sugar filling. This recipe was given to Nicole Kretz of Val-David by her mother, the late Fleur-Ange Vanier Rochon.

> 1 cup (250 mL) brown sugar
> 3 tablespoons (45 mL) all-purpose flour
> 1 cup (250 mL) whipping cream, light cream,
>   or half milk and half cream
> 1 teaspoon (5 mL) vanilla extract or pinch
>   ground nutmeg
> Pastry for double-crust, 8-inch (20 cm) pie
>   (see p. 15)

In a small saucepan, combine brown sugar, flour, and cream. Place over medium heat and bring to a boil, stirring constantly, until thickened. Boil for 2 minutes; remove from heat and stir in vanilla or nutmeg. Let cool.

On a lightly floured board, roll out half the pastry and fit into pie shell and trim edges. Pour filling into pie shell. Roll out remaining pastry to place over filling. Trim pastry, crimp edges, and cut steam vents. Bake in a preheated 375°F (190°C) oven for 40 to 45 minutes or until top crust is golden.

Six servings

TIP: Pastry may be prepared several hours in advance.

GALETTE DE SARRAZIN À SÉRAPHIN

Buckwheat pancakes

This economical recipe is named for a legendary Sainte-Adèle character who kept close guard over his money. The late Fleur-Ange Vanier Rochon of Saint-Jovite recommended making these pancakes with coarsely ground buckwheat and serving them with butter and molasses or maple syrup.

    1 cup (250 mL) buckwheat flour
    1 teaspoon (5 mL) baking powder
    ½ teaspoon (2 mL) salt
    1¾ cups (425 mL) milk
    2 eggs, beaten
    Melted butter

In a bowl, combine flour, baking powder, and salt. Stir in milk and eggs to make a smooth batter. Heat a large, 10-inch (25 cm) pancake pan or heavy frying pan until very hot. Brush with melted butter and pour in ¼ cup (50 mL) of batter; quickly tilt pan to cover bottom with batter. Cook until pancake is lightly browned; turn over and briefly cook the other side. Transfer to a warmed serving platter. Repeat to make other pancakes.

Makes 12 large pancakes

TIP: To make fluffy buckwheat pancakes, substitute 1 cup (250 mL) all-purpose flour for ½ cup (125 mL) of the buckwheat flour specified, increase the baking powder to 3 teaspoons (15 mL), and add 3 tablespoons (45 mL) melted butter to the batter. Pancakes may be made several hours in advance, then reheated in a low oven.

The Laurentian Miser

A penny-pinching character called Séraphin has been a legend in the Laurentians for generations. A pancake made of buckwheat, a grain that would grow in the poor, skimpy soil, was called "Galette de sarrazin à Séraphin," and was originally made only with flour, salt, and water. The character Séraphin was immortalized in the 1940s, when writer Claude-Henri Grignon wrote a radio series about pioneer life entitled *Les belles histoires du pays d'en haut.* This series was later developed for television and became as popular as *The Plouffe Family.* A train, called "Le p'tit train du nord," which had been Curé Antoine Labelle's dream, was part of the Grignon stories. It ceased operating in 1989. On the railway land, a linear park—a 200 km trail running from Saint-Jérôme to Mont Laurier—was opened in 1996 under the original name. The route now attracts cyclists, skiers, and snowmobilers. Information: Association Touristique des Laurentides; (450) 436-8532, (514) 990-5625; www.laurentides.com.

LA MADELEINE GLACÉE
AU MIEL "PAPINEAU"

Madeleines with honey ice cream

Chef Pierre DeLaHaye of Papineauville serves the cuisine of his native Normandy at his restaurant, La Table de Pierre DeLaHaye. Apples, cider, and Calvados are prominent on his menus. Cream and strong, buckwheat-flavoured honey from local honey supplier Jean Marc Peti go into his signature dessert.

> 12 madeleines, either homemade or store-bought*
> Honey Ice Cream (recipe follows)
> Custard Sauce (recipe follows)
> Fruit Sauce (recipe follows)
> Additional fresh fruit in season
> Mint leaves (optional)

*Ladyfingers may be substituted.

Honey ice cream
> 2 cups (500 mL) milk
> ¾ cup (175 mL) strong, dark honey, such as buckwheat
> 4 egg yolks
> 1 cup (250 mL) whipping cream

In a heavy saucepan, combine milk and honey. Place over medium heat, and cook, stirring often, until bubbles form around edge of pan. In a bowl, using an electric mixer, beat egg yolks until lemon-coloured. Pour in cream and continue to beat until mixture thickens. Stir ¼ of the hot milk mixture into yolks, then return yolk mixture to saucepan. Place over low heat, and cook, whisking constantly, until custard thickens enough to coat a wooden spoon; do not let mixture come to a boil. Remove from heat, and strain through a fine sieve. Let custard cool to room temperature, then cover and refrigerate. Freeze in ice cream maker, according to manufacturer's instructions. Makes about 1 quart (1 L) ice cream.

Custard sauce

> 1½ cups (375 mL) milk
> 4 egg yolks
> ⅓ cup (75 mL) granulated sugar
> 2 teaspoons (10 mL) vanilla extract
> 1 tablespoon (15 mL) dark rum

In a medium saucepan, heat milk until piping hot. In a mixing bowl, whisk egg yolks with sugar until smooth. Pour in hot milk in a stream, whisking constantly. Pour mixture back into saucepan and cook over medium heat, stirring constantly with a wooden spoon, until custard thickens enough to coat spoon. Immediately remove from heat; do not let custard boil or it may curdle. Strain through sieve into a bowl. Stir in vanilla and rum. Let cool, then refrigerate, covered. Makes 1½ cups (375 mL) sauce.

TIP: Each part of this recipe may be made the day before and refrigerated.

Fruit sauce

> 2 cups (500 mL) fresh fruit in season
> Instant dissolving sugar

In a food processor or blender, purée fruit until smooth. Strain, if necessary, through a sieve to remove seeds. Sweeten lightly with sugar to taste. Makes about 1¼ cups (300 mL).

To serve, divide custard sauce among 6 large dessert plates. Arrange a madeleine on the sauce, then top with a scoop of ice cream and another madeleine. If using ladyfingers, arrange on each side of ice cream.

Drizzle with fruit sauce and trim each plate with additional fresh fruit and mint leaves, if desired.

Six servings

GASPÉ

Fishermen tell tall tales, and the Gaspé abounds with intriguing stories about the sea. So the story that there were giant cages crowded with lobsters anchored on the ocean floor near Percé rock struck me as just another outlandish yarn, until I met the man who dives down to his watery jail whenever he needs more fresh lobster.

"That's a true one," restaurateurs along the coast assured me. "And it's all legal," said Georges Mamelonet, owner of La Maison des Pêcheurs, the bustling seafood restaurant in Percé harbour, and also the man in the wet suit. Georges explains that, before the local lobster fishing season ends in early July, he fills between 15 and 20 cages with lobsters acquired from local fishermen or his fishing territory off Anticosti Island. Then, all summer long, he keeps about 350 lobsters per cage happy with the scraps from fish he serves in his restaurant, bringing to the surface just the quantities he needs to satisfy his customers with lobster all season.

Along the Percé boardwalk at the graceful old Hôtel La Normandie, Chef François Létourneau is also assured of a summer-long supply of this shellfish, which is so popular on this coast that Percé stages an annual lobster festival each June. François arranges to have a stock of lobsters swimming about in indoor tanks at nearby Sainte-Thérèse-de-Gaspé, allowing him a continual supply to make his favourite lobster dish—a little monk's sack of crisp pastry that holds a delectable mixture of lobster, mushrooms, and pistachios.

Another hidden seafood operation is underway as Gaspé fishermen develop their own system for cultivating mussels in the ocean. Long lines of these mollusks are anchored deep in the waters off the town of Gaspé and in the Bay of Chaleurs. This mussel business, called open-ocean aquaculture, is intended soon to compete with the huge mussel-growing fishery of Prince Edward Island. Already Gaspé mussels by the millions are appearing on the Quebec market.

Fish "farming" was needed in the Gaspé, its fishing industry devastated by the federal closure of the cod fishery. Salmon, trout, and Arctic char are being "farmed" in various locations. But the happiest fishermen in the region are those catching shrimp, which are being fished in vast numbers in the St. Lawrence River. Due to a combination of the reduced numbers of cod, who enjoy feeding on shrimp, and colder Atlantic waters, which shrimp like, Canada has become the number one producer of cold-water shrimp in the world, beating out Norway and Iceland with big catches. The result is that Gaspé shrimp-packing plants are humming, turning out a product that sells all over Canada—the tiny, shelled, cooked, northern shrimp dispensed from supermarket freezers or fish counters. Just how fresh and clean that popular product is was impressed upon me when, having scrubbed up like a surgeon and wearing white from cap to rubber boots, I toured the big Rivière-au-Renard shrimp plant. Thousands of freshly caught shrimp, hauled in ice-filled sacks from the shrimp boats crowding the harbour, were quickly steamed to a pretty pink, then tumbled over rollers to remove their shells, touched with salt to help preserve them, then quickly frozen. It had taken mere minutes to create that convenient product we enjoy on so many salads. Heat them but don't cook them, Chef Desmond Ogden warned after I'd enjoyed his pasta dish with its sauce of shrimp and smoked salmon at his Restaurant Marée Soleil in Gaspé. Since these tiny pink morsels are already cooked, his tip is to add them at the end of cooking, just long enough to heat them through.

Gaspésians used to be called "mangeurs de morue" (cod eaters). They also like herring, often pickled, as well as mackerel, halibut, salmon, and trout. Their bouillabaisse is more closely tied to that of Brittany than the Mediterranean. All traditional dishes are enlivened with salt, part of the region's taste dating from early times when they lived on salted fish and pork.

Times are tough in this region, but food entrepreneurs are devoted to this special corner of Quebec. Bernard Major, who makes goat cheese at his Ferme Chimo in Douglastown, credits his Algonquin Indian background for his patience as he slowly builds his business. Xavier Tiberghien, born like so many original Gaspé settlers in Brittany, was a Montrealer until he came to Gaspé and fell in love with the region. He bakes fine French bread at his bakery in Percé, called Boulangerie La Fournand.

REMOULADE DE CREVETTES ROSE PARMENTIER

Shrimp and potato salad

Chef Desmond Ogden of the Restaurant Marée Soleil in the town of Gaspé uses tiny Nordic shrimp in this salad. Since he's British-born, he refers to the shrimp as prawns.

1 cup (250 mL) diced new potatoes, peeled
1 cup (250 mL) small, cooked Nordic shrimp
¼ cup (60 mL) mayonnaise
1 tablespoon (15 mL) fresh lemon juice
Freshly ground pepper
4 cups (1 L) mesclun or baby salad greens
1 tablespoon (15 mL) finely chopped fresh dill
1 tablespoon (15 mL) finely chopped fresh parsley
2 tablespoons (30 mL) toasted unsweetened
  desiccated coconut (optional)*
Additional shrimp for trim

*To prepare coconut, spread it on a cookie sheet and toast in a preheated 375°F (190°C) oven until golden.

Cook potatoes in boiling, salted water for about 5 minutes or until just tender; do not overcook. Drain and cool. In a bowl, combine potatoes, shrimp, mayonnaise, lemon juice, and pepper. Line 4 ramekins or small custard cups with plastic wrap and pack with potato shrimp mixture. Arrange salad greens on 4 serving plates. Unmould salad onto greens. Trim with dill, parsley, and additional shrimp. Sprinkle with toasted coconut, if desired.

Four servings

TIP: Ramekins may be filled, covered, and refrigerated up to 4 hours ahead.

Salted Herbs

Herbs preserved with vegetables and salt season soups, sauces, stews, and omelettes. Jean-Yves Roy of Sainte-Flavie markets Les Herbes salées du Bas-du-Fleuve throughout eastern Canada. To make it, combine in a large bowl 1 cup (250 mL) of each of the following fresh, finely chopped ingredients: chives, savory, parsley, chervil, celery leaves, and green onions. Stir in 1 cup (250 mL) grated fresh carrots. Have ready from 1/4 to 1/2 cup (60 to 125 mL) coarse salt. Layer 1 inch (2.5 cm) of herb-vegetable mixture in the bottom of a crock or glass bowl and sprinkle with some of the salt. Repeat layers until all of herb-vegetable mixture and salt is used. Cover and refrigerate for 2 weeks. Drain off accumulated liquid and pack herb mixture into sterilized jars. Refrigerate until ready to use. Makes 5 to 6 cups (1.25 to 1.5 L).

TOURTIÈRE LEBOUTILLIER

Aunt Gertie's meat pie

Smelts from the Ice

Ice-fishing is a sport in the Gaspé that has delicious results. My daughter Claire, who lived for several years near the Miguasha park, would look forward to the Bay of Chaleur's freezing each winter so she could venture out onto the ice, either on foot or by snowmobile, to fish for smelts. She'd join the fishermen who had cut a long, narrow hole in the ice so they could lower a net into the ice-cold water. When the tides would start running, the fish would fill the net and the group would haul it up and quickly spread out the catch on the ice. There the tiny fish (about 3 to 4 inches long) would freeze quickly. "We'd push at them with a shovel so they would freeze separately and then, as soon as they were frozen, put them in bags and take them home to the freezer." Come time to eat, she learned to thaw the little fish in a sink full of cold water, then clean them, removing their heads and gutting them. Then she'd dip them quickly in flour, salt, and pepper, and heat a tablespoon (15 mL) of oil and the same amount of butter in a heavy frying pan until sizzling

"That pie is real Gaspé" was the way the late Mabel Reynolds Hyman described this recipe, which she obtained from her lifelong friend, the late Gertrude Leboutillier. Aunt Gertie was a member of a long-time fish-marketing family, who had come originally from the Anglo-Norman island of Jersey. She was considered a "fabulous" cook, says her niece, Kay Leboutillier McCarthy of Montreal. Her spiced beef and pork pie may be frozen unbaked or baked.

> 2 pounds (1 kg) lean ground beef
> 1 pound (500 g) lean ground pork
> 2 onions, chopped
> ¾ cup (175 mL) water
> ¾ teaspoon (4 mL) ground allspice
> ½ teaspoon (2 mL) dried savory
> Salt and freshly ground pepper
> Pastry for 2 double-crust, 9-inch (23 cm) pies
>   (recipe p. 15)

In a large saucepan, combine beef and pork, stirring to blend. Place over medium–high heat and cook, stirring to break up meat lumps, for 7 to 9 minutes or until no longer pink. Place meat in a fine sieve to drain off fat. Return to saucepan and stir in onions, water, allspice, savory, salt, and pepper. Reduce heat to medium–low; partially cover and simmer, stirring occasionally, for 1 to 1½ hours. (Add a small amount of water if mixture boils dry.) Let cool, then refrigerate.

Divide pastry into four rounds. On a lightly floured board, roll out 2 rounds of pastry and fit in bottom of two 9-inch (23 cm) pie plates. Spread meat mixture in pie

shells. Roll out remaining dough and arrange over meat filling. Trim and crimp edges to seal; cut steam vents in top of pastry. Bake in a preheated 425°F (220°C) oven for 10 minutes; reduce temperature to 350°F (180°C) and bake for 20 to 25 minutes or until golden.

Twelve to sixteen servings

TIP: The meat mixture may be prepared several hours in advance. The pies may be completed just to the point they are baked, and frozen for up to one month. Or they may be baked and then frozen. Thaw in refrigerator before baking.

hot. After frying the smelt two to three minutes a side, she'd serve each person panfuls of fish, "as they happen. The cook doesn't eat until all are done," she remembered. She witnessed an even better method at a house with a wood-stove. "They'd get the stove good and hot, sprinkle the stove direct— no pan—with salt, and put the fish right on the salt to cook. They were the best." How do those smelts differ from the ones we buy in our fish counters? "It's like the difference between corn on the cob you've picked that day and corn that's a week old," said Claire.

BOUILLABAISSE LA COULÉE DOUCE

Coulée Douce bouillabaisse

The Celebrated Salmon

Gaspé's famous salmon rivers are still fished by sportsmen who often must throw their small catches back. Filling the demand for this prized fish are salmon farms in the Bay of Chaleurs. The story of this fish is told at the Atlantic salmon interpretation centre at Sainte-Flavie, near the Mitis River, once a great salmon-fishing river. Aquariums, charts, and a film explain why this fish needs protection. Another salmon centre—the Cascapedia River Museum at Saint-Jules, north of New Richmond—explains the time-honoured sport. When Gaspé cooks obtain a good-sized piece of salmon, they like to grill it with bacon or salt pork, or poach it in a lemon-flavoured cream sauce that includes wedges of hard-boiled eggs or sautéed mushrooms and chives. If a whole salmon is to be served, it's often baked with an herb-flavoured bread-crumb stuffing. Salmon pie, salmon croquettes, and salmon soufflé are popular ways to stretch this fish.

In the salmon and trout fishing town of Causapscal in the Matapedia River valley, this Breton-style bouillabaisse soup is regularly served at the Auberge La Coulée Douce. Contents depend on the catch of the day, says innkeeper Vianney Morin, but the soup, made by Chef Sylvie Aubé, is always served in shallow bowls surrounded by hot garlic toast.

½ pound (250 g) salmon steak
½ pound (250 g) halibut steak
½ pound (250 g) cod fillet
1 pound (500 g) raw shrimp, shelled, deveined
¾ pound (375 g) shucked clams
½ pound (250 g) scallops, halved if large
3 tablespoons (45 mL) olive oil
2 onions, chopped
2 cloves garlic, finely chopped
4 ripe tomatoes, peeled, seeded, and coarsely
   chopped
2 tablespoons (30 mL) chopped fresh parsley
1 tablespoon (15 mL) chopped fresh herbs, such as
   marjoram, oregano, basil, and chives
½ teaspoon (2 mL) ground coriander
Salt and freshly ground white pepper
8 cups (2 L) fish stock
½ cup (125 mL) white wine
Hot garlic toast as accompaniment

Cut salmon, halibut, and cod into 1-inch (2.5 cm) pieces. Combine with scallops, clams, and shrimp; set aside.

    In a large stainless steel saucepan or stockpot, heat oil over medium heat and cook onions and garlic, stirring, for

3 minutes, or until softened. Add tomatoes, parsley, herbs, and coriander; season with salt and pepper to taste.

Add fish stock and wine; bring to a boil. Let simmer for 10 minutes. Add seafood mixture; return to the boil. Reduce heat to medium-low and simmer for 5 to 8 minutes or until fish flakes when tested with a fork. Serve in large heated bowls accompanied with garlic toast.

Eight servings

TIP: Fish may be prepared up to 4 hours in advance and refrigerated.

AUMONIÈRES DE HOMARD AUX PISTACHES ET POIVRES VERTS

Lobster in pastry pouches with red pistachio sauce

Where to Stay

A table in the windowed dining room of Hôtel La Normandie in Percé affords the most beautiful view of Percé rock. And, in lobster-fishing season, you can watch the boats at work in the bay from your seaside balcony. It's a comfortable, modernized hotel with exceptional cuisine and meeting facilities. 221 highway 132, Percé; (418) 782-2112, (800) 463-0820; www.normandieperce.com; expensive. For a friendly, family atmosphere, Auberge Le Coin du Banc dates from 1860, has a local chef, good cooking, and long-time owner Lise De Guire, widow of Irish innkeeper Sidney Maloney, at the helm. 315 highway 132 north of Percé; (418) 645-290; moderate. A large, friendly, efficient hotel in what's often called Gaspé Town is

Chef François Létourneau of Hôtel La Normandie in Percé considers this recipe for lobster the hotel's signature dish. Created by his sous-chef, Sylvain Leclerc, the lobster meat is flavoured with a mushroom sauce, enclosed in a small monk's bag of phyllo pastry, baked, and served with a red wine and pistachio sauce.

> ½ cup (125 mL) unsalted butter, melted
> 2 shallots, chopped
> 1 pound (500 g) fresh mushrooms, sliced thinly
> 12 sheets phyllo pastry
> 12 bottled green peppercorns, drained, crushed
> 1 tablespoon (15 mL) pistachios
> 4 lobsters (1¼ pounds/625 g each), cooked, shelled, meat cut in small cubes
> Salt and freshly ground pepper
> Red Butter Sauce with Pistachios (recipe follows)

In a large, heavy frying pan, cook shallots and mushrooms in 2 tablespoons (30 mL) of the butter over medium-high heat, stirring, until mushrooms just start to release their liquid and begin to brown. Place in a strainer set over a bowl to remove excess moisture.

Place one sheet of phyllo pastry on a work surface. Brush lightly with butter. Top with 2 more sheets, brushing each sheet with butter. Place ¼ mushroom mixture in centre and sprinkle with 3 pistachios. Top with ¼ lobster meat and season with salt and pepper. Draw up the corners of the pastry squares over the filling and twist together to close the bundle of pastry firmly. Repeat, making 3 more pastry bundles the same way. Place bundles on a buttered baking sheet. To bake, preheat oven to 300°F (150°C) and bake for 15 to 20 minutes or until pastry is golden. Pour sauce onto 4 warmed plates, add pastry bundles and serve at once.

Four servings

Red Butter Sauce with Pistachios

1½ cups (375 mL) red wine
⅓ cup (75 mL) fish stock
3 shallots, chopped
1½ cups (375 mL) whipping cream
10 bottled green peppercorns, rinsed, drained, and crushed
1 tablespoon (15 mL) pistachios
½ cup (125 mL) chilled butter, cut in small cubes
1 teaspoon (5 mL) fresh lemon juice or to taste

In a medium stainless steel saucepan, combine red wine, fish stock, and shallots. Bring to a boil over medium heat and cook until sauce is reduced to about ¼ cup (60 mL). Add cream, green peppercorns, and pistachios; bring to a boil and cook for about 10 minutes, or until slightly reduced. Using a hand blender at medium speed, blend in butter, one piece at a time, until smooth. Season to taste with lemon juice. Strain sauce through a fine sieve into top of a double boiler set over hot, not simmering, water until ready to serve.

the Quality Inn Gaspé, 178 de la Reine St., Gaspé. Open year-round, it has one of the best dining rooms in the region, called Restaurant Marée Soleil. (418) 368-3355, (800) 462-3355; www.qualityinn.qc.ca; moderate.

TIP: When pastry bundles of lobster are ready to bake, they may be covered and refrigerated for up to 4 hours. Bring to room temperature before baking. Sauce may also be made up to 4 hours ahead, refrigerated covered, then gently reheated.

PERDRIX AU CHOU

Partridge and cabbage

Braising partridge with salt pork in a bed of chopped cabbage is traditional in Norman and Breton cooking. When the late Mabel Reynolds Hyman added apples to her recipe, she was reflecting the Norman background of many of the Gaspé's earliest settlers. Portuguese fishermen visited these coasts for centuries, and the combination of partridge and cabbage is found in Portuguese cuisine. Partridge is now obtainable from specialty farms.

2 partridges (1½ to 2 pounds/750 g to 1 kg each)*
2 tablespoons (30 mL) butter
¼ pound (125 g) salt pork, cubed
1 medium cabbage, coarsely chopped
2 onions, finely chopped
1 clove garlic, finely chopped
2 cooking apples, unpeeled and grated
¼ teaspoon (1 mL) dried thyme
Salt and freshly ground pepper
½ cup (125 mL) water
Large slices of hot, buttered toast

*Farm-raised partridges should require no more than an hour's cooking; wild mature birds may take up to 2 hours to tenderize. Rabbit may be substituted for the partridge called for in this recipe.

Truss partridges by tying legs and wings with string. In a large, deep, flameproof casserole or Dutch oven, heat butter over medium-high heat and brown partridges on all sides. Transfer to a plate. Add salt pork to casserole and cook, stirring, for 5 minutes or until crisp and brown. Drain off excess fat in pan, if desired. Add cabbage, onions, garlic, apples, and thyme; season with salt and pepper to taste. Cook over medium heat, stirring, for 5 minutes. Bury partridges in cabbage mixture. Add water, cover, and cook slowly over medium-low heat for 1½ to 2 hours or until meat is tender.

To serve, cut partridges into serving-size portions and arrange on toast, surrounded by the cabbage mixture.

Six to eight servings

Labels of Good Tastes

Producers of 35 foods native to the Gaspé market their specialties with the logo of a fork and the words "Le Bon Goût Frais de la Gaspésie." Variety extends from fresh fruit and vegetables to fish and caviar, lamb, meat and fish products, maple and honey products, cheese, preserves, and even eggs. Look for the logo in stores and restaurants. A map with shopping information is available in tourist offices or by calling (418) 392-4466. A similar group of 21 producers in the Îles de la Madeleine uses the words "Le Bon Goût Frais des Îles." It has two logos—a fishing boat for seafood and one of the island's square hay ricks for agricultural products. Products include beef, lamb, wild boar, quail eggs, smoked fish, fresh fruit and vegetables, preserves, honey, and cheese. Island stores and restaurants that use these products are listed in a brochure you can get from tourist offices or by calling (418) 986-4550.

MILLE FEUILLES DE FLÉTAN ET SAUMON FUMÉ

Layered halibut and smoked salmon

Chef Desmond Ogden of Restaurant Marée Soleil in the town of Gaspé seasons halibut with salmon that he smokes himself. If the halibut is really fresh, he says, its texture is lighter and its flavour pairs well with the salmon. For wine to accompany this dish, he suggests a chardonnay from Inniskillin of Niagara or the Alsacian wine Hugel et fils.

1¾ pounds (800 g) halibut fillet, cut 1½ inches
  (4 cm) thick
6 ounces (150 g) thinly sliced smoked salmon
Freshly ground pepper
¼ cup (60 mL) unsalted butter, melted
2 tablespoons (30 mL) fresh lemon juice
¼ cup (60 mL) white wine
4 small zucchini, thinly sliced lengthwise
2 tablespoons (30 mL) butter
Salt and freshly ground pepper
2 tablespoons (30 mL) Pernod liqueur*
Beurre Blanc Sauce (recipe follows)

*Another licorice-flavoured liqueur, such as Ricard or Pastis, may be substituted.

Remove bones from halibut and cut into 4 equal pieces. Wrap and place in freezer for about 20 minutes so fish becomes firm enough to slice thinly. Using a sharp knife, slice each piece of fish horizontally into 3 thin slices. Spread 1 slice of smoked salmon on 1 slice of halibut; repeat with remaining fish in the same way to make 4 stacks of alternating fish. Place fish stacks in a deep baking dish large enough to hold the fish in a single layer. Season with pepper; drizzle with melted butter, lemon juice, and white wine. Cover with parchment paper or aluminum foil. Bake in middle of preheated 375°F (190°C) oven for 15 minutes or until fish turns opaque and flakes with a fork. Remove from oven, cover, and keep warm.

In a large frying pan, heat 2 tablespoons (30 mL) butter and cook zucchini just until beginning to soften. Season with salt and pepper to taste. Drizzle with Pernod, and light with match to flame. Serve fish with zucchini and sauce.

Four servings

TIP: The fish stacks may be arranged up to four hours in advance, then covered and refrigerated until ready to bake.

Beurre Blanc Sauce*
¼ cup (60 mL) white wine vinegar
1 small shallot, finely chopped
¼ cup (60 mL) chilled butter, cut in pieces

Using a small, heavy saucepan, cook vinegar and shallot over medium heat until reduced by half. Remove from heat and beat in pieces of butter, one at a time. If necessary, reheat sauce.

*Sauce may be replaced by 1 cup (250 mL) clam juice heated with 1 tablespoon (15 mL) chopped capers and then thickened with 1 tablespoon (15 mL) "beurre manié" (made by blending together 1½ teaspoons [7 mL] soft butter and the same amount of flour), stirred into the clam juice and cooked just until mixture thickens slightly.

POT-EN-POT "TANTE YVONNE" AUX FRUITS DE MER

Seafood pie

In Îles de la Madeleine, family cooks are expert at preparing foods from the deep. This mixed seafood casserole belonging to Yvonne Bouffard of Étang-du-Nord won first prize in a province-wide regional cooking contest sponsored by the Quebec agriculture department in 1983. Mme Bouffard became a successful caterer after her big win. Evaporated milk is traditional on the islands because of the shortage of dairy cows. Dried "fines herbes" called for in the recipes are a combination of tarragon, chives, and parsley.

Pastry

4 cups (1 L) all-purpose flour
8 teaspoons (40 mL) baking powder
1 teaspoon (5 mL) salt
2 teaspoons (10 mL) dry mustard
2 tablespoons (30 mL) chopped fresh parsley
⅔ cup (150 mL) lard
1¾ cups (425 mL) milk

In a bowl, sift together flour, baking powder, salt, and dry mustard. Stir in parsley. Using a pastry blender or 2 knives, cut lard into flour mixture until mixture resembles coarse crumbs. Stir in milk to make a soft dough and gather into a ball. Wrap in plastic wrap and refrigerate for at least 30 minutes.

Divide dough into 2 pieces, one larger than the other. On a lightly floured board, roll out larger piece to a scant ¼-inch (5 mm) thickness and line bottom and sides of a deep, 3-quart (3 L) casserole (8 x 15 x 3 inches or 20 x 38 x 7 cm is recommended). Roll out the remaining pastry to fit the top.

Filling

    1 cup (250 mL) water
    2 cups (500 mL) finely cubed potatoes
    1 cup (250 mL) finely chopped celery
    1 cup (250 mL) finely chopped onion
    1 medium carrot, coarsely grated
    ¼ cup (60 mL) chopped green onions
    1 teaspoon (5 mL) dried "fines herbes" or tarragon
    Salt and freshly ground white pepper
    1 pound (500 g) scallops, cut in small pieces
    1 pound (500 g) lobster meat, cut in small pieces
    1 pound (500 g) raw shrimp, shelled and deveined
    ¼ cup (60 mL) butter
    1½ cups (375 mL) light cream, or 1 can
      (14 ounces/385 mL) evaporated milk
    ¼ cup (60 mL) cornstarch
    ¼ cup (60 mL) water
    Milk
    Olives

TIP: The dish may be assembled up to four hours in advance of baking and refrigerated. Bring to room temperature before baking.

In a large saucepan, combine water, potatoes, celery, onion, carrot, green onion, and fines herbes; season with salt and pepper to taste. Bring to a boil and simmer for 10 minutes or until vegetables are just tender. Add scallops, lobster, and shrimp; cook for 3 minutes or until seafood turns opaque. Remove from heat and stir in butter and cream. In a small bowl, blend cornstarch with water; stir into seafood mixture and place over medium heat, stirring, just until mixture comes to a boil and thickens.

Pour into pastry-lined casserole dish. Brush border of pastry with milk. Add top crust and seal edges with a fork. Decorate crust with 3 pastry cut-outs in the shape of fish. Make steam vents in the shape of waves. Pieces of olives can be used to make the eyes of the fish. Bake in a pre-heated 375°F (190°C) oven for 35 to 45 minutes or until pie crust is golden brown.

Eight servings

MORUE À LA GASPÉSIENNE

Gaspé-style cod

At the comfortable inn Auberge Le Coin du Banc in Percé, Chef Fernand Rehel, who comes from neighbouring Bridgeville, prepares the traditional Gaspé fish dish of poached cod topped with crisp-fried "lardons"—morsels of salt pork—and onions.

> 3 cups (750 mL) water
> 1 cup (250 mL) white wine
> 1 small carrot, finely chopped
> 1 stalk celery, including leaves, chopped
> ¼ cup (60 mL) chopped chives
> Few sprigs fresh parsley
> 1 small bay leaf
> Salt and black peppercorns
> ¼ pound (125 g) salt pork, cut into ½-inch
>   (1 cm) cubes
> 1 Spanish onion, sliced
> 1¼ pounds (625 g) cod fillets*

*Fresh or dried, salted cod may be used. Before cooking, salt cod must be soaked for 24 hours in cold water, then rinsed. Or it may be covered with cold water, brought slowly to a boil, then rinsed.

In a medium stainless steel saucepan, make a poaching liquid by combining water, wine, carrot, celery, chives, parsley, bay leaf, salt, and peppercorns. Bring to a boil; reduce heat and simmer, partially covered, for 30 minutes. Strain through a fine sieve into a bowl and reserve.

In a large frying pan, cook salt pork over medium heat, stirring, for about 5 minutes or until crisp and brown.

The Gaspé Cure

Salting and drying cod is a method of preserving this fish that has remained unchanged on the Gaspé coast since the 16th century, thanks to Basque and Portuguese fishermen who would cross the Atlantic to catch and dry their fish on these same shores. The fish are still cleaned and layered with coarse salt, allowed to marinate, then drained of brine and spread outdoors on racks to dry in the north-westerly Gaspé breezes. The secret to the superior Gaspé product is the wind, says Roch Lelièvre, a Grande-Rivière fish processor. Nova Scotia's winds are moist, so more salt is needed to preserve fish, he explains. Drying quickly, Gaspé fish are tender on the outside, nearly transparent, and able to be stored without refrigeration for up to a year. This fish is considered a delicacy in Mediterranean countries. Making it into a fine meal is easy, Lelièvre says. Soak in cold water and rinse well, then simmer with milk, potatoes, and onions into a stew. Trim with strips of crisply fried salt pork, called "lardons," or bacon.

Transfer to paper towels to drain. Add onions to pan; cook, stirring, for 5 to 7 minutes or until softened and lightly browned.

Place fish in a large shallow saucepan. Pour poaching liquid over fish and place over medium heat; heat slowly until liquid is at a low simmer. Reduce heat and gently poach fish for 7 to 10 minutes, or just until fish is opaque.

Using a slotted spoon, transfer fish to a heated serving platter. Top fish with crisp, cooked salt pork and fried onions.

Four servings

TIP: Poaching liquid may be made several hours in advance, strained, covered, and refrigerated.

TÊTES DE VIOLON À L'AIL

Garlic-flavoured fiddleheads

Gift from the Sea

Along the beaches of the Bay of Chaleurs off Miguasha, a flat, forked seaweed washes up on the sand. Visitors step over it; Gaspésiens collect it to make a soup or dessert. It's called "mousse d'Irlande" (Irish moss), and has a flavour like tapioca. Peter Bujold, whose family are landowners along this shore, compares it to a frayed sponge, green or reddish brown when fresh, creamy white when cooked. It's washed free of sand and shells, then heated in milk until it thickens, much like cream of wheat cereal. The usual flavouring is a dash of vanilla. The cooked mixture is then chilled and served in individual dishes. A dried version is sometimes available in health food shops under the name carageenan. That's the name commercial food processors use, allowing their products to be called natural.

The tiny, curled fronds of ferns, which have gained a reputation as one of Canada's national foods, come mainly from the Matapedia River valley. At Auberge La Coulée Douce in Causapscal, they're steamed, then seasoned with garlic sauce. Chef Sylvie Aubé serves them with the inn's favourite pan-fried fillets of salmon, a remoulade or tartar sauce, and rice pilaf or Duchesse potatoes.

1 pound (500 g) fresh fiddleheads, or 1 package
    (300 g) frozen
¼ cup (60 mL) butter
6 cloves garlic, finely chopped
2 shallots, finely chopped
1 tablespoon (15 mL) soy sauce
1 teaspoon (5 mL) granulated sugar
3 tablespoons (45 mL) white wine

Shake fresh fiddleheads in a paper bag to loosen brown skins; discard skins. In a saucepan, steam fresh or frozen fiddleheads (if frozen, do not thaw first) just until tender, 8 to 10 minutes. Meanwhile, in a large, heavy frying pan, heat butter over medium heat and cook garlic and shallots, stirring, for 2 minutes or until softened. Stir in fiddleheads, soy sauce, sugar, and wine; cook, stirring, for 2 minutes, or until fiddleheads are piping hot. Serve at once.

Four servings

TIP: Fiddleheads may be cooked just until beginning to turn tender, up to 2 hours in advance.

POUDING AU CITRON

Lemon pudding

British cooking is part of the culinary mix in the Gaspé, as this baked lemon dessert from a Percé recipe collection indicates. This recipe for a self-saucing pudding was passed on by the late Mabel Reynolds Hyman, a long-time Gaspé resident, to her daughter, Barbara Maclaren of Montreal.

> 2 tablespoons (30 mL) butter, softened
> ¾ cup (175 mL) granulated sugar
> Juice and grated rind of 1 lemon
> 3 tablespoons (45 mL) all-purpose flour
> 2 eggs, separated
> 1 cup (250 mL) milk
> Pinch salt

In a bowl, cream butter and sugar until fluffy. Stir in lemon juice and rind, flour, and egg yolks, then stir in milk and salt. In another bowl, beat egg whites until soft peaks form. Fold sugar mixture gradually into the beaten whites. Pour into a buttered 1½–quart (1.5 L) baking dish or 6 individual ¾–cup (175 mL) baking dishes. Place in a shallow pan and pour 1 inch (2.5 cm) boiling water into bottom of pan. Place in a preheated 350°F (180°C) oven for approximately 55 minutes for the one large dish, 35 minutes for the individual dishes. Pudding should be firm, lightly browned on top, and starting to pull away from the sides of the dish. Serve either warm or cold.

Six servings

Cod Treats

Cod is the favourite Gaspé fish. Salt cod fish cakes come in patties or bite-sized pieces. In *The Black Whale Cook Book,* a collection of recipes published in Percé in 1948 by Mrs. Ethel Renouf, a recipe from the late Mrs. Clarence Gaul calls for soaking a pound (500 g) of dried salted cod overnight in cold water, then draining and combining the fish with two cups (500 mL) peeled, quartered potatoes. Boil in water to cover until tender, drain well, let dry, then mash with a chunk of butter, a beaten egg, and pepper (no salt), and drop by spoonfuls into a pan of hot oil until browned on both sides. Cod tongues is a traditional appetizer. Ghyslain Chrétien, chef at Restaurant Le Bleu Marine in Carleton, likes to coat the tiny morsels with seasoned flour, then sear them on both sides in hot butter and oil, and bake for five minutes at 350°F (180°C). Serve with a green vegetable or mesclun salad and lemon wedges. An Acadian cod dinner is a "cambuse" or "combuse," in which a whole fish is braised with sautéed strips of salt pork, onions, and potatoes.

POUDING DU CHÔMEUR DE MATANE

Pudding for a budget, Matane style

The recipe for this traditional Quebec dessert comes from a collection published by a women's service group called Le Club Lionnes de Matane, active since 1980 in the St. Lawrence River town. Batter is dropped by spoonfuls to bake, dumpling style, in a hot brown sugar syrup. In the Saguenay region, recipes call for the syrup to be poured over the batter before baking.

Syrup

2 cups (500 mL) brown sugar
2 tablespoons (30 mL) all-purpose flour
3 cups (750 mL) water
1 tablespoon (15 mL) butter

In a saucepan, blend brown sugar with flour; stir in water and butter. Place over medium heat and cook, stirring, until sugar dissolves and butter melts. Pour into a 13 x 9 inch (3.5 L) baking pan.

Batter

2 cups (500 mL) all-purpose flour
⅓ cup (75 mL) granulated sugar
1 tablespoon (15 mL) baking powder
Pinch salt
2 tablespoons (30 mL) butter, melted
¾ cup (175 mL) milk
1 egg, beaten

In a bowl, combine flour, sugar, baking powder, and salt. Stir in melted butter, milk, and beaten egg. Drop large spoonfuls of batter into syrup and bake in a preheated 375°F (190°C) oven for 35 minutes or until dumplings are lightly browned. Serve warm.

Eight servings

TIP: Syrup may be made several hours in advance. Dry ingredients for batter may be mixed in advance.

TARTE AU SUCRE GASPÉSIENNE

Sugar pie, Gaspé style

This dessert, in which brown sugar is combined with rolled oats and evaporated milk in a lattice-topped pie shell, was acquired by the Hyman family of Gaspé from Mme Olympe Boulanger, the late proprietor of one of Percé's oldest inns, the Hôtel Bleu Blanc Rouge, now a B and B. The addition of rolled oats reflects the blend of Anglo-Saxon and French cuisines found in this region. Evaporated milk was traditional in the Gaspé because of the shortage of dairy cows.

> Pastry for double-crust, 8-inch (20 cm) pie shell
>   (recipe p. 15)
> 2 cups (500 mL) packed brown sugar
> ½ cup (125 mL) old-fashioned rolled oats
> 1 small can (160 mL) or ⅔ cup (150 mL)
>   evaporated milk

On a lightly floured board, roll out half the pastry to a 10-inch (25 cm) round and place in an 8-inch (20 cm) pie plate. In a bowl, combine brown sugar and rolled oats; spread evenly in pie shell. Roll out remaining pastry to a 10-inch (25 cm) round and cut into ½-inch (1 cm) strips. Arrange strips on top of filling, in a lattice design, pinching edges to seal. Just before baking, pour evaporated milk carefully through each gap in the lattice topping.

Bake in a preheated 350°F (180°C) oven for 30 to 35 minutes or until bubbling hot and lightly browned. Serve warm or at room temperature.

Eight to ten servings

An Historic Move

One of the Gaspé's dynamic leaders is Joan Dow, who spearheaded the saving and moving of about 20 historic buildings from various parts of the region to create the Gaspésian British Heritage Centre in New Richmond. Joan likes to show a video depicting the slow, steady trucking of big buildings along the highway in 1989 and the creation of a typical village of the period 1780 to 1860. Costumed in the styles of this era, guides lead visitors on a trip back in time to experience life among settlers from the British Isles as they arrived to join pioneers of French Acadian background. You can look up your ancestors at the village art and genealogy centre (located in an antique barn donated by filmmaker Paul Almond, who owns a farm nearby). Walk or ride a shuttle to the general store, school, lighthouse, a garden of old roses, and a restaurant serving British fare. 351 Perron Blvd. West, New Richmond; (418) 392-4487; www.casa-gaspe.com.

BEAUCE

Tucked away in the sugar-maple groves of the Beauce are hundreds of sugar shacks, those homey cabins that warm into action even before the maple sap starts to run each spring. This unique region on either side of the Chaudière River had its cuisine defined early on by the maple. The original dishes of New France, brought south in the early 18th century by settlers from older communities along the St. Lawrence River, were made with plentiful maple syrup, used to glaze a ham or chicken, to sweeten pork and beans or cucumber pickles or an apple dessert.

The first settler to create a farm in the Beauce was Nicolas Comiré, who obtained land in 1737 on the Taschereau seigneury, founded a year earlier. Comiré was soon joined by a dozen other stalwarts, all having to clear the wilderness of trees in order to farm. The name Beauce came originally from a fertile, wheat-growing region of France southwest of Paris. It was aptly applied. Today, many a well-maintained farmhouse dates from those early times, and farms flourish in valleys and on hillsides.

A touch of maple is as much a seasoning as a sweetener, as Cécile Grondin Gamache, a Saint-Marie culinary historian and artist, explains it. Today's chefs add a dash of the syrup to the new and locally raised game birds and boar, bison, and rabbit on their menus.

When the ice begins to go out of the Chaudière and the late winter sun warms the hillsides, it's time for spring maple parties in the "érablières," "cabanes à sucre," and "sucreries," as sugaring-off establishments are variously called. Wood stoves are fired up, the pea soup warmed, and the maple-flavoured specialties served, starting with ham drenched in maple syrup; pork and beans with morsels of salt pork fried as a crisp accent; eggs simmered in the syrup; the "omelette beauceronne" filled with potatoes, crisp-fried salt pork, tomatoes, and Cheddar cheese; crêpes doused in maple syrup; and "tire," the maple taffy that's best enjoyed on a cupful of fresh snow, served along with maple syrup tarts.

Maple is more than folklore in the Beauce. Quebec produces 80 percent of the world's maple syrup, over 28 million litres in a good year, and more each year because of streamlined tree-tapping. Most of the maple harvest comes from the forests of the Beauce. The second area in production is the south shore of the lower St. Lawrence and third is the Eastern Townships. The maple crop is so huge in the Beauce that Quebec's surplus stock of this prized syrup is stored each year in big, stainless steel tanks in the Chaudière valley at Scott-Jonction.

Maple is very much a weather business, maple harvesters explain. Unless a sugar bush, as these forests are called, is treated to warm, sunny days and freezing nights from February through March, the sap doesn't run. Think of the ideal weather for spring skiing and you have the formula. Suffering through a number of winters in the early 1990s when the weather caused such good sap runs that the glut of syrup caused prices to fall below profitable levels, maple producers received government help to set up a system of buying syrup in big years and keeping it to sell in years when the supply is short. They're also tightening up on the quality of a product that is now popular worldwide, including initiating a maple leaf logo for the best Quebec syrup.

Driving about the Beauce, however, you would not think of the importance of maple until you entered a restaurant. Rather, the eye is caught by the manufacturing industry, booming in factory after factory along the Chaudière. The ear hears more English in this region than is usual outside Quebec's big cities, and it's often American-accented. Ever since American general Benedict Arnold passed through in 1775, the U.S. connection has been put to advantage. "The border is near ... the Beauce is very industrialized," Suzanne Vachon, a member of the Sainte-Marie baking family, observed. The inn named after Arnold in Saint-Georges plays on both national tastes in its two restaurants, one specializing in contemporary fresh market cuisine, the other a steakhouse.

SOUPE AUX POIS BEAUCERONS

Pea soup, Beauce style

This hearty soup is a specialty at Auberge Benedict-Arnold in Saint-Georges. It's the most requested dish of American visitors, says Chef Renaud Jacques, who was born in Saint-Elzéar. In summer, he flavours it with fresh herbs. The rest of the year he uses Quebec's favourite salted herbs (recipe p. 167).

TIP: Soup may be prepared and refrigerated or frozen. Defrost in refrigerator before reheating.

1 pound (500 g) dried white pea beans
2 tablespoons (30 mL) butter
1 small onion, chopped
1 small leek, white part only, chopped
8 cups (2 L) cold water
½ pound (250 g) salt pork, in 1 piece
1 meaty ham bone, if available, or ¾ cup (175 mL)
   diced smoked ham
2 tablespoons (30 mL) salted herbs, rinsed in
   cold water (recipe p. 167)
1 large clove garlic, chopped
Salt and freshly ground pepper

Place peas in a large bowl and add water to cover. Soak for 8 hours or overnight; drain. In a large stockpot or saucepan, melt butter over medium heat and cook onion and leek, stirring, for 5 minutes or until softened. Add water, peas, salt pork, ham bone or ham, salted herbs, and garlic. Bring to a boil over high heat. Reduce heat to medium-low and simmer, partially covered, stirring occasionally, for 2 to 3 hours or until peas are tender. Add more water if necessary. Remove salt pork and ham bone, if using. Finely chop salt pork and ham clinging to the bone and return to soup. Adjust seasoning with salt and pepper to taste.

Eight servings

POTAGE DU BLÉ

Corn soup

This fresh corn soup from Renaud Jacques, chef at Auberge Benedict-Arnold in Saint-Georges, is rich and creamy. It may be made with frozen or canned corn kernels, but it won't have the same delicate sweetness the fresh corn provides.

> 2 cups (500 mL) water
> 2 cups (500 mL) milk
> 4 cups (1 L) fresh corn kernels
> 1 teaspoon (5 mL) salt
> 2 tablespoons (30 mL) butter
> ⅓ cup (75 mL) chopped celery
> ¼ cup (60 mL) chopped onion
> ¼ cup (60 mL) chopped leek, white part only
> 2 tablespoons (30 mL) all–purpose flour
> ½ cup (125 mL) whipping cream
> Salt and freshly ground pepper

Place water in a large saucepan and bring to a boil. Add milk, corn, and salt; cook for about 3 minutes or until corn is just tender. Strain cooking liquid into a bowl and set corn aside. In same saucepan, melt butter over medium heat and add celery, onion, and leek. Cook, stirring, for 5 minutes or until vegetables are softened. Stir in flour and cook until bubbly. Add reserved corn cooking liquid and cook, stirring constantly, until mixture comes to a boil. Reduce heat and simmer, partially covered, for 15 to 20 minutes. Remove from heat and add reserved corn. Purée in batches in food processor or blender until smooth. Return to saucepan and add cream; adjust seasoning with salt and pepper to taste. Place over medium heat until piping hot.

Four to six servings

Where to Stay

A restored old house with modern, motel wings, Auberge Benedict-Arnold, just outside Saint-Georges, is large, comfortable, and friendly and has an excellent restaurant serving fresh regional cuisine, and also a steakhouse. Not far from the Maine border, it's popular with American business visitors, who may be aware that Arnold was an 18th century American general. He was welcomed and his army offered food by the French settlers when he travelled north in 1775 in what turned out to be a failed attempt to conquer the British at Quebec City. 18255 Lacroix Blvd., Saint-Georges; (418) 228-5558, (800) 463-5057; www.aubergearnold.qc.ca; conference facilities; moderate.

SALADE D'HIVER

Wintertime salad

In days gone by, raw vegetables were salted and bottled in a vinegar-sugar mixture, then stored in a cold pantry. In winter, this "salad" provided a change from pickles or root vegetables from the cold storage bin. Mariette Vachon of Saint-Marie contributed this family recipe to a collection published by the rural women's group Cercle de Fermières in her town.

> 8 pounds (4 kg) firm, ripe tomatoes, peeled and chopped
> 6 large onions, chopped
> 2 green peppers, cut in small cubes
> 1 red pepper, cut in small cubes
> 1 stalk celery, chopped
> ¼ cup (60 mL) coarse pickling salt
> 2 cups (500 mL) vinegar
> 2 cups (500 mL) granulated sugar
> 2 tablespoons (30 mL) mustard seeds

Place tomatoes, onions, peppers and celery in a large bowl; stir in salt. Cover bowl with a cloth and let stand overnight.

The next day, drain vegetables thoroughly. In a saucepan, heat together vinegar, sugar, and mustard seeds just until sugar dissolves, then cool. Pour over drained vegetables and mix well. Ladle evenly into hot sterilized jars. Seal, cool, and refrigerate or store in a very cool place for at least 7 days before using.

Makes 5 to 6 one-pint (500 mL) jars

History Recreated

Imagining pioneer times is easy at the Village des défricheurs (settlers' village), a recreated 19th century community in Sainte-Prosper, east of Saint-Georges. It's composed of 12 buildings that were moved to the site, several original, plus some recreations. A manor house displaying folk art and antiques, farmhouses, a schoolhouse, blacksmith's shop, sawmill, general store, and a barn that is used as a summer theatre, can all be visited on guided tours. Open in summer. 3821 highway 204; (418) 594-6009 or 228-5362; www.belin.qc.calvillage-musee. Further east in Sainte-Rose-de-Watford is a 1910 general store and historical museum at 600 Principale St., open in summer, (418) 267-5434. A miniature village of 75 period houses, many of them models of actual Beauce buildings, is open in summer in Saint-Georges. Take highway 204 East and 58th Ave. (418) 228-8796.

RAGOÛT DE PATTES DE LARD AUX GRANDS-PÈRES

Pork hocks stew with dumplings

Seigneurial Style

The first seigneury in the Beauce was granted in 1736 to the Taschereau family of Quebec City, who had originally emigrated from Touraine in west-central France. The imposing white, pillared house, the second seigneurial manor to be built there, was completed in 1809. It faces the Chaudière River just north of Sainte-Marie, and includes a 1778 family chapel. Down through the centuries, the Taschereaus produced two judges, one on the Supreme Court of Canada, a premier of Quebec, and a cardinal. Continuously inhabited by the family, it's now the home of Miriam Taschereau, a Quebec City lawyer. Manoir Taschereau is run year-round as a deluxe B and B. Groups may reserve for a tour of the house, led by costumed actors playing Seigneur Jean-Thomas Taschereau (1778-1832) and his servants. 730 Notre-Dame St. North, (418) 387-3671; www.comsearch-can.com/manoir.htm.

This spicy dish, with Quebec's traditional combination of cinnamon and cloves, is on the menu at special events in the Beauce, Christmas in particular.

> ¼ cup (60 mL) browned flour*
> 2 pork hocks
> 2 upper pork hocks
> 2 tablespoons (30 mL) butter
> 3 medium onions, coarsely chopped
> ¼ pound (125 g) salt pork, in 1 piece
> 1 bay leaf
> Salt and freshly ground pepper
> ½ teaspoon (2 mL) cinnamon
> ¼ teaspoon (1 mL) ground cloves
> Dumplings (recipe follows)

*Sprinkle all-purpose flour in heavy frying pan and cook, stirring, over medium heat, until flour turns the colour of brown sugar, about 5 minutes. Or use a commercial brand.

Scrub pork hocks under cold water and pat dry. In a large, cast-iron casserole or stockpot, melt butter over medium-high heat and brown pork on all sides. Add cold water to cover; add onions, salt pork, bay leaf, and salt and pepper to taste. Bring to a boil, skimming off any foam that rises to the surface. Cover and reduce heat to medium-low; simmer for 3 hours. Remove pork hocks and salt pork; discard salt pork. Cut meat into bite-size pieces, discarding any fat and bones. Strain stock through a sieve into a large bowl, then return to casserole or stockpot. Add pork pieces, cinnamon, and cloves. Place over medium heat. Blend browned flour with enough water to make a paste and blend into stew. Bring to a boil, stirring, until sauce thickens. Adjust seasoning with salt and pepper to taste.

Meanwhile, prepare dumpling batter. With the stew at a gentle simmer (reduce heat if necessary), add spoonfuls of batter to stew, then cover with lid or tightly cover with heavy-duty aluminum foil. Simmer for 10 minutes; remove lid and simmer for 10 minutes more. Serve immediately.

Six to eight servings

TIP: Stew may be made the day before up to the point you strain the stock, and return it to the casserole with the meat and spices. Refrigerate. Brown the flour. The next day, skim off fat on surface of stew and continue with the recipe.

Dumplings

1 cup (250 mL) all-purpose flour
1 tablespoon (15 mL) baking powder
¼ teaspoon (1 mL) salt
3 tablespoons (45 mL) shortening
½ cup (125 mL) milk

In a bowl, combine flour, baking powder, and salt. Cut in shortening using a pastry blender or 2 knives until mixture resembles coarse crumbs. Using a fork, stir in milk to make a soft, sticky dough.

CROÛTES DE FILET MIGNON DE PORC AU FROMAGE OKA

Pastry-wrapped pork tenderloins with Oka cheese

This recipe is from Chef Jean-Philippe Renaudin of Restaurant La Table du Père Nature in Saint-Georges. He flavours the pastry-wrapped pork tenderloins with a sauce of maple-flavoured cranberries. He likes to serve the dish with zucchini strips quickly sautéed in oil.

2 pork tenderloins (1½ pounds/750 g)
2 tablespoons (30 mL) all-purpose flour
Salt and freshly ground pepper
1 tablespoon (15 mL) each butter and vegetable oil
1 package (14 ounces/397 g) frozen puff pastry, defrosted
7 ounces (200 g) Oka cheese, rind removed, cut into 8 thin slices
1 egg yolk
Cranberry Maple Sauce (recipe follows)

Cut each pork tenderloin in half crosswise to make 2 equal-size pieces. Place flour on a plate and season with salt and pepper. Lightly roll pork in seasoned flour, shaking off excess. In a large, heavy frying pan, add butter and oil and heat until sizzling hot. Add pork and brown on all sides. Remove from pan and let cool slightly.

Cut puff pastry into 2 pieces. On a lightly floured surface, roll each piece into a 14 x 7 inch (35 x 18 cm) rectangle. Cut each piece in half to make 2 squares, measuring 7 x 7 inches (18 x 18 cm).

Arrange 1 piece of cheese on each of the pastry squares. Top each with pork and again with a slice of cheese. Brush edges of pastry with water and wrap pastry around pork, pinching edges to seal. Arrange seam side down on baking sheet. In a bowl, beat egg yolk with 1 tablespoon (15 mL) water. Brush pastries with egg yolk mixture. Bake in a preheated 350°F (180°C) oven for 15 to 20 minutes or until pastries are golden.

To serve, drizzle sauce on 4 heated serving plates and top with pastry-wrapped pork.

Four servings

Cranberry Maple Sauce

1 tablespoon (15 mL) butter
1 shallot, finely chopped
3 tablespoons (45 mL) maple syrup
¾ cup (175 mL) white wine
¾ cup (175 mL) cranberry juice
1 teaspoon (5 mL) cornstarch (optional)
Salt and freshly ground pepper
⅓ cup (75 mL) dried cranberries

In a small stainless steel saucepan, heat butter over medium heat and cook shallot for 2 minutes or until softened. Add maple syrup and cook until reduced and slightly caramelized. Add wine and cook over medium-high heat until reduced by half. In a measuring cup, blend cranberry juice with cornstarch; stir into sauce and bring to a boil, stirring, until slightly thickened. Add dried cranberries and season with salt and pepper to taste.

TIP: Sauce may be made 3 hours in advance, then removed from heat and set aside. An hour ahead, pork may be prepared up to the point it is wrapped in pastry and arranged on baking sheet. When ready to bake, brush pastry with egg mixture. Bake pastry-wrapped pork and reheat sauce.

POITRINE DE POULET AU SIROP D'ÉRABLE

Maple-baked chicken breasts

Beauce Menu

Potage du blé (p. 190)

Corn soup

Poitrine de poulet au sirop d'érable (p. 196)

Maple-baked chicken breasts

Whipped potatoes with chives

Steamed broccoli

Poires pochées au miel et au gingembre (p. 204)

Pears poached with honey and ginger

Chicken and pork are often baked or braised in maple syrup in the Beauce. This easy recipe for chicken breasts can also be used with a whole, cut-up broiler-fryer chicken. It's from the collection of Jeanne d'Arc Nadeau, long-time proprietor of Le Danube Bleu reception hall in Sainte-Marie and a cookbook author.

> 4 single bone-in chicken breasts
> ¼ cup (60 mL) all-purpose flour
> Salt and freshly ground pepper
> 2 tablespoons (30 mL) butter
> ½ cup (125 mL) maple syrup
> 1 teaspoon (5 mL) dried savory leaves
> ½ teaspoon (2 mL) dried thyme leaves
> ¼ teaspoon (1 mL) crushed dried sage
> 1 onion, thinly sliced
> ½ cup (125 mL) water or chicken stock

Place flour in a heavy plastic bag and season with salt and pepper. Lightly dredge chicken in flour mixture, shaking off excess. In a large, cast-iron frying pan or flameproof casserole dish, heat butter over medium-high heat until bubbling. Add chicken breasts and brown on both sides. Pour maple syrup over and sprinkle with savory, thyme, and sage. Arrange onion slices over top and add water to pan. Wrap a double layer of foil over pan handle if not ovenproof, and place pan in preheated 350°F (180°C) oven. Bake, basting chicken occasionally with pan juices (add more water or stock, if needed), for 50 to 60 minutes, or until tender when pierced with a fork.

Four servings

TIP: Chicken may be
prepared 2 hours in advance
up to the point where it is
ready to bake.

FÈVES AU LARD

Pork and beans

Jarrets Noirs

The moist and muddy banks of the Chaudière River helped give the Beaucerons the nickname "jarrets noirs" (black hocks), in use to this day. This river is notorious for its spring floods. The nickname is traced to the muddy feet the inhabitants would acquire during flood season. Another story is that the term refers to the black feet, or hocks, of the horses that pulled their owners' carts, or "charettes," along the river. They'd be heading to market in Lévis, selling their wares and buying such essentials as salt, spices, and molasses. The admission from a Beauceron that he or she is originally from the Beauce is usually said with pride. One of the region's treasures to be boasted about is at Notre-Dame-des-Pins—a red-painted covered bridge erected over the Chaudière in 1929 and believed to be the longest such bridge (154.5 metres) in Quebec.

A basic of Beauceron cuisine, this traditional dish may be flavoured either with molasses and brown sugar or with maple syrup, says Sainte-Marie culinary historian Cécile Grondin Gamache. When her region's favourite game bird, partridge, is available, she uses maple syrup in her beans and tucks the breasts of three partridges into the centre of the pot. A breast of chicken may be substituted for the partridge.

> 1 pound (500 g) dried white navy beans
> ½ cup (125 mL) molasses*
> ¼ cup (60 mL) brown sugar*
> 1 teaspoon (5 mL) salt
> ¼ teaspoon (1 mL) freshly ground pepper
> 1 teaspoon (5 mL) dry mustard
> 2 medium onions, chopped
> ½ pound (250 g) salt pork**
> 3 breasts of partridge or 1 breast of chicken
>   (optional)

*The molasses and brown sugar may be replaced with ¾ cup (175 mL) maple syrup.
**Salt pork may be left whole and removed when beans are cooked, then sliced and served. Or it may be sliced before adding to the beans and incorporated into the dish.

Place beans in a stockpot or large saucepan and add cold water to cover. Soak for 8 hours or overnight; drain. Return beans to stockpot and cover with 12 cups (3 L) fresh, cold water. Bring to a boil over high heat, reduce heat to low, and simmer, covered, for about 1 hour or until beans have softened slightly.

Drain beans, reserving cooking liquid. In a heavy casserole with a cover, combine beans, 6 cups (1.5 L) cooking liquid, molasses, brown sugar, salt, pepper, mustard, and onions. Tuck pork and partridge breasts, if using, into centre of dish. Cover and bake at 250°F (120°C) for 6 to 8 hours. Remove cover for final hour of baking. Add more bean cooking liquid or water during baking, if needed. To serve, arrange partridge breasts on heated platter; surround with beans.

Six servings

TIP: Baked beans may be frozen for up to 2 months. Defrost in refrigerator, then reheat.

OEUFS DANS LE SIROP D'ÉRABLE

Eggs in maple syrup

Maple Products

Until the 1950s, the average family in this sugar maple region consumed an estimated 200 pounds (100 kg) of maple products a year, half of it in the form of maple sugar. Sugaring-off workers would use fresh maple sap to make tea. In the early days, woodsmen boiled the sap in cauldrons over a campfire. Later, shacks and wood stoves were used, and they would make "viande boucanée," rinsing slabs of salt pork in brine, then hanging the meat from the rafters of the sugar shack. Vapours from the boiling sap and the maple log fire would gradually impregnate the meat. Today most harvesting is done with plastic pipes and evaporators. Maple sugar has become a delicacy, to be snapped up in the spring at roadside stands and markets. Maple vinegar and maple jelly are specialty ingredients. And three maple syrup liqueurs have been launched on the market, one flavoured with whisky, another with rum, a third with Grand Marnier.

This rich, sweet recipe for eggs and maple syrup makes the ultimate brunch dish in the Beauce. It appears during the spring maple run. In the old days, if the thick maple taffy known as "tire" was cooking on the stove, a sugar shack cook might drop the eggs into this confection instead of using the usual bubbling hot syrup. In Beauce kitchens today, the eggs are often beaten before they are cooked, and sometimes a teaspoonful (5 mL) of butter is dropped into the syrup before the eggs. This recipe belongs to Mariette Scully Bourque of Notre-Dame-des-Pins.

> 2 cups (500 mL) maple syrup
> 3 eggs
> ⅓ cup (75 mL) milk
> Pinch salt

In a heavy saucepan, bring maple syrup to a boil over medium heat just until syrup thickens. Meanwhile, in a bowl, beat eggs lightly with milk and salt.

When syrup has thickened, reduce heat to low. Using a wooden spoon, drop spoonfuls of the egg mixture into hot syrup. Cook for 2 to 3 minutes or until eggs are set. Immediately remove saucepan from heat and place it in a larger pan of cold water to cool slightly. Spoon eggs into serving bowls and drizzle with syrup.

Six servings

POUDING AUX POMMES AU SIROP D'ÉRABLE

Apple maple pudding

Apples and maple syrup are natural partners in the Beauce. This easy recipe was obtained from an elderly family cook by Sainte-Marie culinary historian Cécile Grondin Gamache.

> 3 large or 6 small cooking apples, peeled, cored, and thickly sliced
> 1 cup (250 mL) maple syrup
> 1 egg
> 1 tablespoon (15 mL) melted butter
> 2 teaspoons (10 mL) lemon juice
> ½ cup (125 mL) all-purpose flour
> 1 teaspoon (5 mL) baking powder
> Pinch salt
> ½ cup (125 mL) raisins
> Unsweetened whipped cream (optional)

Place apples in a greased 8-inch (20 cm) square glass baking dish; pour over ½ cup (125 mL) of the maple syrup. Stir to coat well, and spread in an even layer.

In a bowl, beat the egg and stir in butter, lemon juice, and remaining ½ cup (125 mL) maple syrup. In another bowl, combine flour, baking powder, and salt. Stir the dry ingredients into maple mixture to make a smooth batter. Fold in raisins. Spoon batter evenly over apple slices. Bake in a preheated 375°F (190°C) oven for 30 to 35 minutes or until top is lightly browned. Serve warm with unsweetened whipped cream, if desired.

Six servings

GÂTEAU JOS. LOUIS

The Jos. Louis Cake

The size of a big hockey puck, the Jos. Louis, Quebec's favourite "snacking cake," was launched in 1933 by Sainte-Marie baker Rose-Anna Vachon. She used old baking powder cans as moulds, baked the cakes in a wood stove, and named them after Joe Louis, the champion U.S. boxer. When the cake started selling south of the border in the 1960s, lawyers became concerned that the boxer might challenge the trademark. So Rose-Anna and her husband Joseph-Arcade Vachon renamed the cake Jos. Louis, ostensibly after two of their six sons, Joseph and Louis. The boxer never

Jos. Louis Cakes

Home-made versions of this popular chocolate cake with vanilla or chocolate filling turn up in recipe collections throughout the Beauce. A product of the giant Vachon bakery at Sainte-Marie, the so-called "snacking cake" was launched in 1933. Home recipes use a drop-cookie method and, sometimes, a marshmallow filling. The bakery cake is made automatically with a diameter of 3 1/2 inches (9 cm). To achieve a symmetrical look and a light texture, I adapted a recipe belonging to Mariette Scully Bourque of Notre-Dame-des-Pins to the muffin tin.

Cake

½ cup (125 mL) butter, softened
½ cup (125 mL) granulated sugar
2 eggs, beaten
1½ teaspoons (7 mL) vanilla extract
1 cup (250 mL) milk
1 tablespoon (15 mL) white vinegar
1 teaspoon (5 mL) baking soda
2 cups (500 mL) all–purpose flour
¼ cup (60 mL) unsweetened cocoa powder
1 teaspoon (5 mL) baking powder
½ teaspoon (2 mL) salt
Vanilla Filling (recipe follows)
Chocolate Icing (recipe follows)

Grease 24 medium muffin cups. In a large bowl, cream butter with sugar until fluffy. Beat in eggs and vanilla. Measure milk into a large measuring cup and stir in vinegar, then baking soda. In another bowl, sift together flour, cocoa powder, baking powder, and salt. Stir dry ingredients into creamed mixture, alternating with milk mixture. Spoon batter into muffin cups, filling only half full. Bake in a preheated 350°F (180°C) oven for about 10 minutes or until a tester inserted in centre comes out clean. Cool for 10 minutes in pans. Turn out onto rack and cool completely.

Vanilla filling

2 egg whites
½ cup (125 mL) granulated sugar
Pinch salt
2 tablespoons (30 mL) water
1 teaspoon (5 mL) vanilla extract

In the top of a double boiler set over boiling water, combine egg whites, sugar, salt, and water. Using an electric mixer, beat until stiff peaks form, about 3 to 4 minutes. Remove from heat and beat in vanilla.

Chocolate icing

¼ cup (60 mL) butter, softened
¼ cup (60 mL) unsweetened cocoa powder
⅓ cup (75 mL) light cream
1 teaspoon (5 mL) vanilla extract
1 cup (250 mL) sifted icing sugar (approximate)

In a bowl, cream butter with cocoa powder. Blend in cream and vanilla. Stir in enough icing sugar until icing is of spreading consistency.

To assemble, slice cakes in half horizontally. Fill with Vanilla Filling and spread tops and sides with Chocolate Icing.

Makes about 24 medium-sized cakes

sued. A novel about the family success story, *Le rêve de Rose-Anna Vachon,* was published by Roger Lacasse in 1993. When Canada Post issued its millennium year 2000 stamps, one was inscribed "J.A. Vachon Fils, Pâtissiers" and bore photographs of the family and nine of the cakes. "I received a birthday card with the Vachon stamp on it," said Montrealer Suzanne Vachon, granddaughter of the late Rose-Anna. "It's a very moving experience to have the portrait of your family on a stamp."

POIRES POCHÉES
AU MIEL ET AU GINGEMBRE

Pears poached with honey and ginger

This dessert from Chef Jean-Philippe Renaudin of Restaurant La Table du Père Nature in Saint-Georges flavours pears with honey and ginger and adds a sabayon sauce made with honey wine.

1 cup (250 mL) honey
1 cup (250 mL) water
Juice of ½ lemon
1 tablespoon (15 mL) finely chopped fresh
   gingerroot
4 firm but ripe Bartlet or Anjou pears, peeled, cored

Sabayon
6 egg yolks
2 tablespoons (30 mL) honey
½ cup (125 mL) honey wine (mead) or white wine
Petals of edible flowers

In a small saucepan, combine honey, water, lemon juice, and gingerroot; bring to a boil. Add pears and reduce heat to medium–low; poach for 20 to 25 minutes, or until tender when pierced with a knife. Using a slotted spoon, transfer pears to a bowl. In a stainless steel mixing bowl, combine egg yolks, honey, and honey wine and place over a saucepan of simmering water. Using an electric mixer, beat for about 3 minutes or until foamy and thickened. Arrange pears on 4 serving plates and top with warm sabayon sauce. Trim with flower petals.

Four servings

TIP: Poach pears 2 hours in advance and let stand, covered.

INDEX

RECIPE CREDITS

The following recipes were adapted from these cookbooks and are reprinted with the permission of the publishers:

Beauce: "Ragoût de pattes de lard aux grands-pères," "Fèves au lard," "Pouding aux pommes au sirop d'érable" from *Les Plats d'autrefois* by Cécile Grondin Gamache. Scott-Jonction, Québec: Imprimerie Bô-Modèle Inc., 1986.
"Poitrines de poulet au sirop d'érable" from *Vingt ans de réussite culinaire* by Jeanne d'Arc Nadeau. Sainte-Marie, Québec: privately published, 1983.
"Oeufs dans le sirop d'érable," "Gâteau Jos. Louis" from *Les meilleures recettes de Maman Mariette* by Mariette Scully Bourque. Notre-Dame-des-Pins, Québec: privately published, 1987.

Côte du Sud: "Crème aux pommes" from *Les meilleures recettes québécoises d'autrefois* by Suzette Couillard and Roseline Normand. L'Islet-Sur-Mer, Québec: Diffusion Suzette Couillard Inc., 1986.
"Pouding aux pommes et à l'érable" from *L'ordinaire 2* by Thérèse Beaulieu-Roy. Mont-Joli, Québec: Les Ateliers Plein Soleil Inc., 1979.

Eastern Townships: "Ragoût d'agneau" from *100 Recettes d'Antan* by Cercle de fermières de Cowansville. Cowansville, Québec: Imprimerie Cowansville, Inc., 1976.
"Salade aux pissenlits," from *Nos recettes préférées* by Cercle de fermières de Sainte-Edwidge, Compton, Québec: Les Editions Compton, 1986.

Gaspé: "Pouding du chômeur" from *Les recettes de mes amies* by Club Lionnes de Matane. Matane, Québec: privately published, 1982.

Laurentians-Outaouais: "Tarte à la ferlouche" from *Les recettes des fermières du Québec*. Chomedey, Laval, Québec: Les Editions Penelope, Inc., 1978.
"Gâteau à la citrouille de Lochaber" from *Cent ans de tradition culinaire québécoise* by Le Cercle des Fermières de Thurso. Saint André-Avallin, Québec: Les Editions de la Petite-Nation Inc., 1984.

Mauricie-Lanaudière: "Soufflé aux navets," "Asperges marinées," from *Au pays de Laviolette 350 fourchettes* edited by Peggy Lafrenière. Trois-Rivières, Québec: Imprimerie Saint-Patrice enr., 1983.
"Oatmeal lace cookies," "Crêpes normandes" from a recipe book published privately by Le Cercle AFEAS de St. Zéphirin de la Tuque. La Tuque, Québec: 1979.

Montérégie: "Applesauce bread" from *Recipes* by Hemmingford Branch, Quebec Women's Institutes, Hemmingford, Quebec: privately published, 1972.

Québec: "Crêpes à Nicole" from *Recettes de pommes de terre à la mode de chez nous*. Laprairie, Québec; Club optimiste de Saint-Ubalde, Editions des Deux Mondes, 1984.
"Pâté aux poireaux" from *Les Délices de l'Île*. Île d'Orléans, Québec: privately published, undated.

Saguenay-Lac Saint-Jean: "Soupe à l'ivrogne" from *150 Recettes pour le Saguenay-Lac St-Jean à cuisinier* by Micheline Mongrain-Dontigny. La Tuque, Québec, privately published, 1988.
"Croustade aux bleuets" from *Le pinereau: l'art culinaire au saguenay-lac saint-jean* by Cécile Roland Bouchard. Montreal: Les Editions Leméac, 1971.

PHOTO CREDITS

Page 5 *Lunch en plein air.* Courtesy of Elizabeth Lambert.

Page 6 *Fernand Cana-Marquis, a leek grower of Sainte-Famille.* Courtesy of Julian Armstrong.

Page 8 *L'Initiale restaurant in Quebec City.* Courtesy of Clement Allard/The Gazette.

Page 11 *Bernard Monna with his black currant liqueur.* Courtesy of Julian Armstrong.

Page 16 *Baskets of blueberries with a local classic,* Maria Chapdelaine, *perched on top.* Courtesy of Julian Armstrong

Page 18 *Typical roadside signs.* Courtesy of Julian Armstrong.

Page 24 *Chef Claude Cyr.* Courtesy of Julian Armstrong.

Page 29 *Sculptures by the water in Sainte-Flavie.* Courtesy of Julian Armstrong.

Page 30 *Straw fisherman at Sainte-Flavie.* Courtesy of Julian Armstrong.

Page 32 *Chef Richard Duchesneau with scallops.* Courtesy of Julian Armstrong.

Page 34 *Fresh from the oven at Folles Farines.* Courtesy of Julian Armstrong.

Page 35 *Folles Farines bakers Valérie Jean and Claude Saint-Pierre.* Courtesy of Julian Armstrong.

Page 36 *Not for eating but for viewing.* Courtesy of Julian Armstrong.

Page 37 *Les Rochers, Sir John A. Macdonald's summer retreat.* Courtesy of Meredith Fisher.

Page 43 *Baker Hervé Gobeil.* Courtesy of Julian Armstrong.

Page 45 *Auberge des Peupliers at Cap à l'Aigle.* Courtesy of Auberge des Peupliers.

Page 49 *Hikers overlook Charlevoix scenery.* Courtesy of Heiko Wittenborn/Tourisme Québec. heikow@sympatico.ca

Page 65 *Chef Denise Cornellier displays her specialty.* Courtesy of Peter Martin/The Gazette.

Page 69 *Chef Normand Laprise at work.* Courtesy of Pierre Obendrauf/The Gazette.

Page 72 *McIntosh apples at the Atwater Market.* Courtesy of Richard Arless Jr./The Gazette.

Page 77 *A springtime garden.* Courtesy of Elizabeth Lambert.

Page 78 *Ken Taylor with his crop.* Courtesy of Pierre Obendrauf/The Gazette.

Page 87 *L'Abbaye Saint-Benoît-du-Lac.* Courtesy of Jocelyn Boutin/Tourisme Québec.

Page 89 *Cooking up a 10,000-egg omelette in Granby.* Courtesy of Richard Chagnon/The Gazette.

Page 96 *A round barn in the Eastern Townships.* Courtesy of Benoit Charlifour/Tourisme Québec.

Page 109 *Chef Diane Tremblay in her garden.* Courtesy of Julian Armstrong.

Page 111 *The little white house in Chicoutimi.* Courtesy of Julian Armstrong.

Page 115 *The Normandin gardens.* Courtesy of Julian Armstrong.

Page 124 *Isabelle Dupuis tends Sir Wilfred Laurier's restored home.* Courtesy of Gordon Beck/The Gazette.

Page 133 *Iron sculpture at Forges-du-Saint-Maurice.* Courtesy of Parks Canada.

Page 135 *Springtime thaw.* Courtesy of Elizabeth Lambert.

Page 140 *Beekeeper René Déprès at Saint-Benoît honey farm.* Courtesy of The Gazette.

Page 145 *Rivière la Diable near Tremblant.* Courtesy of Pierre-Philippe Brunet/Tourisme Québec.

Page 147 *Chef Anne Desjardins with fresh herbs.* Courtesy of L'Eau à la Bouche, Saint-Adèle.

Page 151 *A country road in autumn.* Courtesy of Elizabeth Lambert.

Page 169 *Drying salt cod in Percé.* Courtesy of Julian Armstrong.

Page 174 *A partridge in its natural setting.* Courtesy of Jean-Pierre Huard/TourismeQuébec.

Page 181 *Salting cod in Grande-Rivière, Gaspé.* Courtesy of Julian Armstrong.

Page 185 *Rafts on the shore at Saint-Flavie.* Courtesy of Julian Armstrong.

Page 195 *Tree-tapping in the Beauce.* Courtesy of Yvon Thibodeau/Beauce office de tourisme et congrès.

Page 196 *A cabane à sucre with the resident helper.* Courtesy of Yvon Thibodeau/Beauce office de tourisme et congrès.

Page 201 *Making maple taffy.* Courtesy of Jean Pierre Huard/Tourisme Québec.

Page 202 *Jos. Louis cakes.* Courtesy of Vachon bakery, Sainte-Marie. *Regional menus photo.* Courtesy of Jocelyn Boutin/Tourisme Québec